THE UGLY FACE
OF
INSTITUTIONAL RACISM

A True Story of an
Overseas Trained Teacher

VUPENYU waMWAMBA

ISBN 978-1-7361332-4-8 (paperback)
ISBN 978-1-7361332-5-5 (eBook)

Copyright © 2021 by VUPENYU waMWAMBA

All rights reserved. No part of this publication may be reproduced, distributed, or transmitted in any form or by any means, including photocopying, recording, or other electronic or mechanical methods without the prior written permission of the publisher.

Printed in the United States of America

> RACISM IN THE UK'S EDUCATION SECTOR: Illustrated with documentary evidence

> We paid £3525 recruitment fee to Simply Education, a teacher recruitment agency for him to become a permanent member of staff.
> **(Jane Crow: The Head teacher)**

> Your overseas qualifications, and experience is not recognized here. That is the law.
> **(Jane Crow: The Head teacher)**

> The School Salary policy is not applied to Overseas Trained Teachers in this school

> Jane (head teacher) further said, Although he understands he is an OTT, we fully accepted other qualifications which are recognized by National Recognition Information Certificate (NARIC) as valid, we do not recognize your teaching qualifications here.
> **(Linda Scuder: governor)**

> Mrs Crow (the head teacher) went on to explain that it is your teaching qualification which is not recognized in this country according to national policy.
> **(Andy Morgan, Chair of governors)**

> Did the Employment Tribunal serve the interests of the Whites in Mr Fox's case? An impartial judge would ask the obvious question: **Why did you employ him in the first place if you did not recognize his qualifications and their country of origin?**

The Race Relations Act 1965 was the first legislation in the United Kingdom to address racial discrimination. **This act outlawed discrimination on the grounds of colour of skin, race, or ethnic or national origins.**

The issue of racism in the education sector in the United Kingdom is a public phenomenon following the evidence presented to Parliament in a report by teachers' unions. In 2017, Runnymede, NASUWT, and Act for Racial Justice published the report 'Visible Minorities, Invisible Teachers: BME Teachers in the Education System in England', which presented the NASUWT big-question survey findings, alongside other research, evidencing poor experiences across the school system for BME teachers, with discrimination and unequal treatment starting early in teachers' careers, with lower pay on average than peers, amid a pervasive culture of racism. Head teachers flout with impunity their school salary policies and teachers pay and conditions service. An overseas teacher is not paid as well as his or her white counterpart. Overseas-trained teachers are not given the same promotion opportunities as their white counterparts. This manuscript is compiled against that backdrop of a research which was conducted by teachers' unions and activists. The true story of Mr Fox (a fictitious name) is quite harrowing. In his own words, Mr Fox said, 'If you dare challenge prejudicial discrimination and slave mentality perpetrated by head teachers, you risk summary dismissal and lifetime ban.' The reader is reminded that head teachers have created a 'Dismissed Teachers Registers', which can be accessed only by head teachers. Once the teacher has been listed on that particular register, he or she will not be employed again anywhere in the UK. Racial discrimination against black and minority ethnic teachers is a scourge which threatens the values of a multicultural and multiethnic British society. It dehumanises people and create stressful experiences which lead to premature death. The 'Me Too' movement in the United States of America has changed the political and social profile of that country. The big and most powerful men have been called to account for their predatory behaviour as women stand up to them. In a similar vein, this biography of Mr Fox, who was dismissed and banned from teaching for life for trying to challenge racism and racial discrimination at his workplace, is a wake-up call to black and minority ethnic groups to stand up in unison to name and shame the few racists in the United Kingdom. The experiences of Mr Fox, an overseas-trained teacher, is harrowing but needs to be told as it is.

CHAPTER 1

BREACH OF CONTRACT AND RACIAL DISCRIMINATION

Mr Fox (Morrison Ngwenya) was posted to Cardinal Newman Secondary School by Simply Education Recruitment Agency as a supply teacher. Towards the end of his supply contract, the head teacher, Mrs Jane Crow, and the head of department, Ms YPY, persuaded him to stay on and join them as a permanent teacher. The head teacher paid Simply Education, the teacher recruitment agency, a very large sum of money as a recruitment fee for Mr Fox to become a permanent member of staff **(See doc 1)**. In paying this large sum of money, Mr Fox did not realize that the head teacher had literally bought the teacher for that sum of money.

A contract was signed between Mrs Jane Crow and Mr Fox **(docs 2 and 3)**. From here on, the teacher lost his rights. As the reader will see below, the teacher was stripped of his qualifications, and yet he had been employed as an overseas-trained teacher (OTT), with qualifications which are equivalent to UK qualifications **(See doc 4)**. At the time Mr Fox was employed, the school had twelve non-EEA teachers, who had trained overseas **(See doc 5)**. Some of those teachers obtained their qualifications at the same institution as Mr Fox, and at least three of them qualified the same year as Mr Fox **(See doc 5)**. This education background is important because it is the centre of discrimination.

VUPENYU waMWAMBA

that makes it clear what elements of the lesson went well and what was in need of development. Anyone reading these lesson observations can see that they were written by people who cared about the Claimant and were trying to help him improve.

71. At page 367a there is an attendance record since 2007 of the Claimant's sickness absence. The breakdown of illness is as follows:

    - 2007-2008 – 1.7 days medical over 3 separate occasions
    - 2008-2009 – 0.6 days absence for medical over 2 occasions
    - 2009-2010 – 0 days absence for medical
    - 2010-2011 – 0.2 days absence for medical
    - 2011-2012 – 4 days absence for medical over 2 occasions

72. The facts above do not appear to be in keeping with a man who claims that he is suffering from a fatal illness, needs to pay off his mortgage because he risks leaving his family destitute and needs to pay for a full time carer.

The Claimant's *"response"* to the School's defence

73. As part of the proceedings, the Claimant supplied the tribunal with a response to the School's defence (pages 19a-19f). My comments with respect to this document are set out below.

74. The Claimant was not appointed in his first interview as he was the weaker candidate. The two candidates who were appointed were both Black Africans. They were also practicing Catholics which gave them an additional advantage and that is something that Voluntary Aided faith schools are legally entitled to consider for posts such as this (an RE teacher). We are not disputing that his pay was previously at UQ10 with Mark Rutherford School in Bedford. <u>When we appointed him he was working for Simply Education, a Supply Agency. We therefore had to pay them £3,525.00 as a recruitment fee for the Claimant becoming a permanent member of staff</u>. After gaining QTS he was moved onto the main scale in line with STPCD.

75. Mrs Slawinski was correct in explaining that in order to become accepted by a university to go through QTS, the student's degree normally has to include at least 50% content in the subject the student is training to teach. This is not a regulation invented by the School.

Doc 1 - Bought for £3525

The Ugly Face of Institutional Racism

THE CONTRACT

Date: 5 June 2007

CARDINAL NEWMAN

CATHOLIC SCHOOL
A Specialist Science College

Warden Hill Road
Luton
Bedfordshire   LU2 7AE
Tel: (01582) 597125
Fax: (01582) 503088
email: Cardinal.Newman.Admin@luton.gov.uk

Dear Morrison Mwamba Ngwenya,

Post of RE Teacher   (Scale UQ 10)

On behalf of the Governors I am pleased to offer you the above mentioned post with effect from June 1st 2007. The first day of the teachers' term is September 3rd 2007, pupils return on the 5 September 2007.

This offer of appointment is subject to the National Conditions of Service applicable to all teachers and also to any special provisions relating to Roman Catholic Voluntary Aided Schools. Chief among these is active support for the school's particular ethos as outlined in the prospectus and other key documents. It is also subject to satisfactory references and any special provisions of your individual job description which, after consultation with yourself, may from time to time be amended by the Headteacher and Governors.

All teaching appointments in Luton are subject to a satisfactory medical assessment and also to Form X (police record) clearance.

I shall be pleased to receive your written acceptance of this post as soon as possible. May I offer you the good wishes of myself and the whole Governing Body. I hope you will find your work at Cardinal Newman Catholic Secondary School happy, successful and rewarding.

Yours sincerely

pp. A Morgan
Chair of Governors

Headteacher
Mrs Jane Crow

Deputy Headteachers
Mrs Fleur Musonda

Doc 2 - Contract

VUPENYU waMWAMBA

To: The Chair of Governors

CARDINAL NEWMAN CATHOLIC SCHOOL
A Specialist Science College
Warden Hill Road
Luton
Bedfordshire LU2 7AE
Tel: (01582) 597125
Fax: (01582) 503088
email: Cardinal.Newman.Admin@luton.gov.uk

Date: 5th June 2007

Dear Sir

Thank you for your letter of ....5th June........ offering me the post of ....RE Teacher........ with effect from ....1st June 2007....

I accept the post and have noted the date of the first day of term.

Yours sincerely

[signature]

dteacher
Jane Crow
uty Headteachers

Doc 3 - Contract

The Ugly Face of Institutional Racism

UK NARIC
National Recognition Information Centre for the United Kingdom

ORIEL HOUSE, ORIEL ROAD, CHELTENHAM, GLOUCESTERSHIRE, GL50 1XP. HEAD OF UK NARIC DR. CLOUD BAI-YUN
Services for Individuals: Tel. +44 (0) 870 990 4088   Services for Organisations: Tel. +44 (0) 870 990 1661   Fax +44 (0) 870 990 1560   WEBSITE: www.naric.org.uk

Mr Morrison Mwamba Ngwenya
59B Ford End Road
Bedford
MK40 4JF

31 July 2006

NARIC Reference Number: 1941651826 Morrison Mwamba Ngwenya

Dear Mr Ngwenya,

Thank you for your recent enquiry.

Further to this, I am now able to confirm the following:

1

Country of Qualification:	South Africa
Title of Award:	Master of Education in Didactics
Awarding Institution:	University of South Africa
Year of Completion:	1999
Assessment:	Is considered comparable to British taught Master's degree standard
Additional Information:	Together with a Certificate of Registration issued by the South African Council for Educators, qualifies the holder to teach in South Africa.

2

Country of Qualification:	Zimbabwe
Title of Award:	Postgraduate Diploma in Educational Technology
Awarding Institution:	University of Zimbabwe
Year of Completion:	1997
Assessment:	Is considered comparable to British Postgraduate Diploma standard

www.uknrp.org.uk

REGISTERED IN ENGLAND AT 30 ST GILES, OXFORD, OX1 3LE. 2405026

www.uknec.org.uk

Doc 4 - NARIC Qualifications p1

VUPENYU waMWAMBA

UK NARIC
National Recognition Information Centre for the United Kingdom

ORIEL HOUSE, ORIEL ROAD, CHELTENHAM, GLOUCESTERSHIRE, GL50 1XP. HEAD OF UK NARIC DR. CLOUD BAI-YUN
Services for Individuals: Tel: +44 (0) 870 990 4088 Services for Organisations: Tel: +44 (0) 870 990 1561 Fax +44 (0) 870 990 1560 WEBSITE www.naric.org.uk

3
Country of Qualification:	South Africa
Title of Award:	Postgraduate Diploma in Tertiary Education
Awarding Institution:	University of South Africa
Year of Completion:	1997
Assessment:	Is considered comparable to British Postgraduate Diploma standard

4
Country of Qualification:	Zimbabwe
Title of Award:	Graduate Certificate in Education
Awarding Institution:	University of Zimbabwe
Year of Completion:	1987
Assessment:	Is considered comparable to British Postgraduate Certificate standard
Additional Information:	Qualifies the holder to teach at Secondary level in Zimbabwe subject to State requirements.

5
Country of Qualification:	Zimbabwe
Title of Award:	Bachelor of Arts General Degree
Awarding Institution:	University of Zimbabwe
Year of Completion:	1985
Assessment:	Is considered comparable to British Bachelor (Ordinary) degree standard

We are aware that, in order for applications for teacher training to be considered, GCSE equivalence in certain subjects is required. For your information, the Cambridge School Certificate / GCE O level from Zimbabwe may be considered comparable to GCSE (grades A*-C) / Credit Standard Grade standard when grades of 1 to 6 (or A-C) are awarded.

If you qualified to teach outside the European Economic Area your qualification will not automatically be recognised in England. If you are interested in gaining Qualified Teacher Status please contact the Overseas Trained Teacher advice line on 01245 454 321 or ott@ttainfo.co.uk / www.tda.gov.uk

Please note that section 21 of the South African Council for Educators Act 2000 requires that every Educator contemplated by the Act must register with the Council before appointment to a teaching post and that no person may be employed as an Educator by an employer unless that person is registered with the Council. We therefore recommend that to confirm eligibility to teach in South Africa a certificate of registration with the South African Council for Educators is also presented.

REGISTERED IN ENGLAND AT 30 ST GILES, OXFORD, OX1 3LE. 2405026

www.uknec.org.uk

Doc 4 - NARIC Qualifications p2

The Ugly Face of Institutional Racism

UK NARIC
National Recognition Information Centre for the United Kingdom

In addition to your Letter of Comparability you may wish to receive a UK NARIC Certificate of Comparability. This provides you with your comparability statement in a certificate format which is often required by employers or other institutions. This Certificate is an entirely optional service. The cost of the Certificate is £23.50 (including all taxes) per qualification, payable by cheque or postal order to ECCTIS Ltd. Please contact the UK NARIC stating your reference number and the name of award should you require a NARIC Certificate.

The service provided by UK NARIC, although based on informed opinion, should be treated only as guidance.

I hope this is of assistance.

Yours sincerely

C Miles

Charlotte Miles
Information Officer

Doc 4 - NARIC Qualifications p3

List of Overseas Trained Teachers (OTT)/Black and Minority Ethnic (BME) or Non EEA teachers employed at Cardinal Newman Catholic Secondary School since 2000.

Name	Year for Initial Teacher Training (ITT)	Country where (ITT) qualifications obtained	Year obtained QTS	Main Scale after QTS	Experience In years
	1985	Zimbabwe	2004	M6	19
	1998	Jamaica	2007	M5	9
	1995	Ghana	2006	M5	11
	1985	Zimbabwe	2008	M3	23
	1998	Jamaica	2005	M6	7
		Zimbabwe	2006	M5	
	1985	Zimbabwe			
	2000	Nigeria	2009	M3	9
	2005	Zimbabwe			
	1995	Ghana			
		Pakistan?			
		Nigeria			
		Ghana			
		South Africa			
		India			
		Ghana			
		South Africa			
		Kenya			
		Ghana			
	1985	Zimbabwe			
	1986	Zimbabwe			
	1985	Zimbabwe			
	1987	Zimbabwe			
	1986	Zimbabwe			
	1985	Zimbabwe			
	1987	Zimbabwe			

The head teacher refuses to disclose details of these teachers because of inconsistencies in which they were awarded salary being Non-EEA.

Doc 5 - List of OTTs

Soon after joining Cardinal Newman Secondary School, Mr Fox enrolled for qualified-teacher status (QTS), an accreditation course, which he completed in one year, thereby meeting the statutory requirements to be recognised as a qualified teacher and reap the benefits of that status, like any other teacher in the United Kingdom. Mr Fox's salary was supposed to be adjusted soon after completing QTS, according to the School Teachers' Salary Policy (2005), paragraph 3 (i) starting salary; paragraph 3 (ii) on experience; and paragraph 4 (i) on experience, from unqualified 10 (£23,331.00) to M6 (£30,148.78); however, it did not change **(For references See appendix, refer to salary policy page 139)**. The head teacher Mrs. Jane Crow, refused to adjust Mr Fox's salary according to the sections of the salary policy quoted above. When Mr Fox enquired why his salary had not been adjusted according to the school salary policy, Mrs. Jane Crow advised him to follow the school's grievance procedure. Following the school's grievance procedure required him to present his grievances to the head teacher in the first instance, which he did.

Mr Fox reminded the head teacher about the implications of meeting the requirement of a contract that he had signed and the obligations on her part to pay him according to the salary policy she had given him. He also reminded her that when he signed that contract, she had given him the Staff Handbook, which is a standard practice as these are the working documents. Mr Fox reminded her that the handbook had, among other documents, the following policy documents:

- Child Protection Policy,
- Code of Conduct Policy, and
- Health and Safety policy, Equality policy, and Grey School Salary Policy

Mrs Jane Crow was further reminded of the contents and obligations of their salary policy. By refusing to apply the salary policy, she was in breach of the contract. Throughout the deliberations, as Mr Fox followed the school grievance procedure, and leading to his dismissal, Mrs. Jane Crow (the head teacher), Mr. Andy Morgan (representing the governors), the Luton Borough Council (LBC)'s human resources department (HR), and the BBC's legal department pretended and indeed denied the existence of a salary policy, which is referred to throughout this book.

The reader will therefore be referred to sections of this document, showing when these authorities either made misleading statements, denied its existence, or, worse still, quoted the wrong instruments altogether. The reader should be made aware that salary policies of all schools in England and Wales try, as much as possible, to mirror the National Teachers' Pay and Conditions of Service. School-salary policies, which are compiled by the body of governors, are standard, and they strive to mirror that Teachers' Pay and Conditions of Service. They are expected to lay out how they are going to pay their teachers, recognising

- the requirements of the school's pay and conditions document;
- the school's delegated budget;
- their current staffing structure; and
- the legislation in respect of equal opportunities and equal pay.

Of particular interest is the section which stipulates starting salary. Of interest is section 3 (STARTING SALARY OF NEW ENTRANTS) which stipulates the obligations of the governors. The governing body has adopted the local agreement in respect to the assessment of teachers' pay. The starting salary for all new entrants to the teachers' pay spine, without previous teaching or relevant industrial, professional, or research experience, will be at point M1(See Salary policy). They are required to be very clear about the starting point and the subsequent pay levels, including awards, so that there is no misunderstanding between the teacher and the host school. The document also points out that for the new entrant to the profession who has experience which may count towards salary, points will be awarded in respect of (a) teaching service and (b) industrial, professional, and research experience, considered to be of value in the performance of the teacher's duties on the basis of one point in respect of each complete period of two years. New entrants to the profession are required to complete the equivalent of three terms of satisfactory induction. Successful completion enables continuous eligibility of employment as a teacher. The instrument also points out that qualified teachers taking up a new appointment, or who re-enter teaching after a break in service, will be paid on a point on the teachers' pay spine no lower than the point on which they were last being paid, calculated by reference to the teacher's qualifications and experience. This calculation will be carried out whether the teacher was previously employed on a regular full-time or part-time or occasional supply basis. Where the governing body employs a qualified classroom teacher who was last employed as a head teacher or assistant head teacher, appointment will be to the first point of the upper pay spine (plus any additional allowances), U1, provided that the teacher has worked in that capacity for a minimum of three years or was employed in that capacity prior to 1 September 2007. A classroom teacher who was previously employed as an AST will revert to the point of the upper pay spine (U1).

Mr Fox was highlighting that particular section which points out that the governing body will award up to six points for experience. A teacher (including a part-time or occasional supply teacher) will be eligible for an experience point for each school year in which the teacher has taught for part of the twenty-six weeks, or was due to but was prevented from doing so for reasons of sickness, maternity, or some other absence acknowledged by the governing body. Experience as a qualified teacher within an Education Action Zone, at an MOD school, or as an AST will be taken into account in determining eligibility for experience points. The governing body acknowledges that it has the discretion to withhold a point from a teacher where the teacher's performance is deemed to be unsatisfactory **(See appendix, Salary policy).**

The head teacher, Mrs. Crow, refused outright to accept that Mr Fox deserved to be remunerated according to the stipulations of the salary policy as referred to above. These are signs of slave labour in the United Kingdom. Black and minority ethnic teachers have no negotiating rights. They depend on the goodwill of head teachers and not on the requirements of the policies in place. When Mr Fox compared his salary to colleagues who had the same qualifications as his and who had completed qualified teacher status for the same period as him, the head teacher argued that his colleagues had been placed at a higher level because they belonged to subject areas which were in short supply of teachers, and so they were given recruitment and retention incentives.

Mr Fox showed Mrs. Crow the section of the salary policy that deals with recruitment and retention incentives. That section is clear. It says in considering the award of recruitment and retention incentives, the governing body will have regard for fluctuations in the supply of suitably qualified and experienced teachers. Decisions on the allocation of recruitment and retention incentives will be based on objective evidence. Mr Fox argued that the policy points out that in the event of a standard advert being unlikely to produce credible field for the post, an advert will be run which will offer additional incentives. If practicable, the standard advert will run. These incentives can include any one of or combination thereof, such as 2.5 per cent of the substantive salary on a fixed-term basis (maximum duration three years). That teacher will be helped with removal expenses, will be helped with rent, and will be provided with a laptop computer. Head teachers seem to have a lot of powers to make life-changing decisions about a teacher. They exploit BME teachers in two or more ways. They dictate what salary they can offer you, and then they give you the option to choose. In this type of scenario, the head teacher can pay the teacher what she pleases. That way, they can serve on their budget. Another scenario is one in which you are not recognised by the school because your contract is not recognised. The school has no dealings with the teacher. They instead talk to you through the agency. In this scenario, the head teacher avoids meeting any other financial obligation which may be due to the teacher. The head teacher receives the full support of the body of governors to exploit BME where possible in order to accommodate their budget.

The Conversation between Mr Fox and Mrs. Crow.

The school grievance resolution procedure required Mr Fox to discuss his grievances with the head teacher in the first instance. Only when they had reached a deadlock would he appeal to the governors. Mr Fox carried a copy of the salary policy referred to above to Mrs. Crow's office.

> Mr Fox: Mrs. Crow, after going through the school salary policy and having compared my salary with other teachers who completed QTS the same time as I did, I feel that you placed me at the wrong pay point. I joined this school from other schools who had placed me at point 10 of the unqualified (£23,331) **(See appendix)**. After completing QTS, my salary has not changed as I hoped it would.
>
> Mrs. Crow: You still need to complete your induction; then we will see your so-called qualifications and experience.
>
> Mr Fox: Yes, I will complete the induction, but my salary should have changed because I have completed QTS.

Mrs. Crow: We are going to consider the residuals of your GCSE classes who passed with As and Bs. That is when your salary will be adjusted.

Mr Fox: I am not happy. I do not see how all this comes into my entitlement, which is clearly outlined in the school's salary policy (paragraph 3 (i); 3 (ii); and 4 (i) above). Besides, there is inconsistency in the manner in which you applied that instrument.

The reader should notice that the head teacher, Mrs . Crow, was in breach of the school salary policy, and for that reason, she was evading the issue of the school salary policy above. Secondly, her first response explains why Mr Fox had been forced to do an induction. Induction had nothing to do with salary. In her responses, Mrs. Crow was beginning to show signs of discrimination in her language. In saying, 'Complete your Induction; then we will see your so-called qualifications and experience,' Mrs. Crow was demeaning Mr Fox's qualifications. Mr Fox informed the author that the head teacher was beginning to be arrogant. He could feel that their relationship had changed from being a professional one to a master-and-servant relationship. A couple of months after he had started discussing with Mrs. Crow his salary, the school recruited another teacher, a Mrs Bee, whom Mr Fox had met with in his previous school, Mermaid Community School. Mr Fox informed the author that when he left Mermaid school, Mrs Bee was doing QTS, which she had just completed, and had been placed at M5. Mrs Bee was an overseas-trained teacher (OTT). Mr Fox knew Mrs Bee to be fifteen years his junior. Mr Fox informed the author that it is not easy to approach other BME staff to find out how they were treated when they completed QTS, but he did. Mr Fox felt strongly that there was something wrong. He made another appointment to see the head teacher.

The Ugly Face of Institutional Racism

Mr Fox: Mrs. Crow, there are many people who are fifteen years my junior who are getting the same salary as me or even higher. When I looked at my salary and compared it with one of my juniors whom I met at my last school, I feel there are some discrepancies.

Mrs. Crow: What you are getting is the correct salary. Your former school (referring to Mermaid Community School where he was teaching the year before) was turned into an academy. They have more money than us, so they can afford to pay their teachers any amount of money.

Mr Fox: Mrs. Crow, I have shown you sections of the pay policy which you gave me when I signed this contract and have also pointed out to inconsistencies and irregularities in your interpretation and application of the salary policies, but you do not want to acknowledge your mistake. I am frustrated that you are treating me that way. What you are saying about Mermaid Community School is not true and has nothing to do with salary issues.

Mrs. Crow: After all, your overseas qualifications and experience are not recognised here **(See appendix)**.

Mr Fox said he was shocked and surprised that Mrs. Crow was making such a claim about his qualifications and experience, when he had been employed as a qualified teacher with the same qualifications as other overseas-trained teachers. The author could see Mr Fox's eyes rolling with tears. Shaking his head in disbelief, Mr Fox informed the author that he went over the details about how he was employed, explaining that his qualifications were rated as equivalent to UK qualifications by NARIC and that they were at the same level as the rest of the OTT in school, which Mrs. Crow knew. He said he reminded Mrs. Crow that the attitudes she was expressing in some of the statements she made pointed to racial discrimination.

Mr Fox said that while he was still negotiating his salary with the head teacher, he received a school email, in which Mrs. Crow circulated the school self-evaluation form, as they were preparing for an inspection. He noticed that it had misleading information about his status **(See appendix, School Self Evaluation)**. Mr Fox's experience was recorded as four years (4) and yet he had been teaching for twenty two years (22). He politely contacted Mrs. Crow about an error in the information provided in the SEF to visitors and to all members of staff. He reminded her that when the school employed him, he was employed as an overseas trained teacher and that he did not train to become a teacher in the UK. He further pointed out that he had more than twenty years' experience, so their records in the SEF were wrong. He politely asked the head teacher to correct that information and resend to all members of staff so that they had the correct picture of my situation. Mr Fox received another shocker. With a sobbing tone, Mr Fox told me that the head teacher repeated a racist remark she had made earlier on. She claimed that the school can only write in the experience from the point of view of when he gained QTS in this country as his previous qualifications were not recognised in this school **(See appendix).**

At this point, Mr Fox realised that, like a slave, he had lost his rights, his qualifications, and his humanity. This is happening in the United Kingdom. With the backing of the governors, this institution was beginning to treat Mr Fox like a slave. Why would she refuse to recognise the teacher's qualifications? The reader should notice that Mrs. Crow was rejecting Mr Fox's qualifications, and yet he was employed on the basis of the same qualifications. If the governors were not of the same mindset, they were supposed to rein in on the head teacher and correct the situation. There is no way Mr Fox could have been admitted by the university to do QTS if his qualifications had not been recognised in the United Kingdom. The reader is reminded that the reason for not paying Mr Fox correctly was that his qualifications were obtained overseas. Yet, ironically, in a period of ten years, the school had employed twenty-two overseas-trained teachers (OTTs), twelve of whom were still in school. Mr Fox said at this point it became clear that the motivation for discriminating him was racial above all else. The author could hear Mr Fox sobbing, saying, 'I am beginning to realise that when the head teacher told me that she had paid Snail Teacher Recruitment Agency £3,525 as recruitment fee for me to become a permanent member of staff, she literally meant she had bought me from an agency so she was not prepared to pay him more.'

These are some of the contradictions found in the education system in the United Kingdom. Mr Fox informed me that two or more BME teachers he had spoken to were not surprised because they too had experienced similar attitudes. The author consoled him and encouraged him to continue.

Mr Fox informed the author that when he exhausted the school grievance policy, until he reached the Employment Tribunal after three years of negotiating. Mr Fox further informed the author that in all those three years, it was becoming clear that the institution exploiting him was far larger than he had thought. It comprised Mrs. Crow (the head teacher), Mr. Morgan (representing the governors), the Luton Borough Council (LBC)'s human resources department (HR), and the BBC's legal department, all of whom pretended and indeed denied the existence of a salary policy which has been referred to above. Mr Fox said he did not know that racism was so deeply entrenched in the United Kingdom. Mr Fox asked a rhetorical question. 'Do you see that white people instinctively support Mrs. Crow although they know that she is breaking the law?'

The Employment Tribunal was not impartial either. Mr Fox presented documentary evidence of racial discrimination to the tribunal, but they ignored that evidence and chose instead to sympathise with the head teacher. Mr Fox informed the author that, at the tribunal, he had argued that he had been forced to do an induction, which she knew he was not supposed to do. He further argued that he was targeted among the eleven teachers who were recruited the same time as him, because the school had paid recruitment fees of £3,525. Mr Fox informed the author that when he made reference to these other eleven teachers, the head teacher unwittingly produced a table below which was intended to illustrate how she had arrived at the salaries of said teachers. The reader is reminded that Mrs. Crow was trying to illustrate the years of experience of each teacher and how they were paid. This table is meant to illustrate the inconsistencies in the application of the salary policy. Mr Fox said it was shocking to notice the judge was ignoring this kind of evidence. The judge could have asked very simple questions, like, 'When you completed your initial teacher training, how long had you been teaching?' Instead, the judge dismissed this evidence below.

Newly-qualified teachers employed the same time as the claimant

Name	Start date at Grey School	Starting pay scale	Qualified date	Revised pay scale	Trained at Grey School	Completed NQT at Grey School	Ethnicity
1	01/09/08	UNQ3	Jul 10	M3	Yes	YES	W B
2	01/07/10	UNQ 4	Jul 10	M1	No	YES	W B
3	01/07/10	UNQ4	Jul 10	M1	No	YES	W B
4	01/09/10	UNQ4	Jul 11	M2	YES	Currently	W B
5	01/09/09	UNQ5	Jul 10	M3	YES	YES	W B
Mr Fox	01/06/07	UNQ10	Jul 08	M3	YES	YES	**BME**
7	01/09/06	UNQ6	Jul 09	M3	YES	YES	W B

8	01/09/08	UNQ3	Jul 11	M1	NO	YES	A B
9	01/09/08	UNQ3	Jul 11	M1	NO	YES	W B
10	01/07/10	UNQ4	Jul10	M2	NO	YES	W B
11	01/09/10	UNQ4	Jul10	M3	NO	YES	WB

WB = White British, AB = Asian British, BME = Black Minority Ethnic

The information in the table above suggests to readers that the complainant in row 6 (Mr Fox) received his initial teacher training (ITT) at Grey school in 2007, and yet he completed his ITT in 1985 and had been employed as a qualified teacher since. Mr Fox breathed deeply and said loudly, 'This kind of racial discrimination and bullying is mind-boggling.' Mr Fox informed the author that the table he was showing me excluded other teachers who, when they completed QTS the same period, were placed at M5-M6. The head teacher had no way of justifying the discrepancies in the awarding of salary among five people who had similar qualifications and the same experience as his. Mr Fox and I agreed that the table referred to above showed that the salary policy had not been applied properly.

The head teacher's argument in the table above is that Mr Fox had no qualifications to be recognised when he joined Grey School. The table shows that Mr Fox was placed in the same category with teachers who were twenty-two years or more his junior. The head teacher could not justify the discrepancy in the table above if she was applying the salary policy.

- Teacher number 1 in the table completed ITT in 2008, and their QTS in 2010 was placed at M3 = £24,048.
- Teacher number 5 completed ITT in 2009, and their QTS in 2010 was placed at M3 = £24,048.
- Teacher number 6 completed his ITT in 1985, and his QTS in 2008 was placed at M3 = £24,048.
- Teacher number 7 completed his ITT in 2006 and was placed at M3 = £24,048.

It was clear that the head teacher, Mrs. Crow, was using whim to pay teachers, not the salary policy.

The same table above shows that seven teachers with initial teacher training (ITT) were employed the same time as the complainant. Of the seven teachers, the complainant is the only minority black African; the rest are white British. Mr Fox argued that all the teachers were employed on the basis of their Initial Teacher Training Qualifications, either trained in the UK or overseas, which were recognised by NARIC. Why would the head teacher turn around and claim that they no longer recognised his qualifications? Their experience ranged from 0 to 22 years of teaching, hence the wide range of starting pay scale of Unqualified 1–Unqualified 6(10). On completing QTS, each one of them was moved to the Main Scale (M1–M6) according to previous years of experience.

The table shows that PG (white British) was moved to M3 because he had three years in teaching. The same table shows that all white British had their one year or two years' experience considered. The same table sadly shows that Mr Fox's qualifications were not recognised; that is why his start date is recorded as the date when he joined Cardinal Newman School. Mr Fox asked the head teacher if there was another factor she had considered in awarding him his salary after completing QTS, and she did not list any. The judge kept quiet. When Mr Fox asked Mrs. Crow if she had a separate salary policy for the BME teachers, she said she did not have any. When she was asked why there was that discrepancy, and she kept quiet. The judge also kept quiet about it. The ugly face of institutionalised racism. Is the justice system just? Is there any point in having anti-discrimination laws when the justice system does not enforce them?

Mr Fox cleared his throat and said, 'My life is ruined. The school allowed this case to drag on and on, knowing that it would be dismissed at the Employment Tribunal for being out of time.' The ET rejected all the documents which were presented as evidence of race discrimination, arguing that it was an afterthought on the part of Mr Fox, and then dismissed the case. Mr Fox said that he realised at that point that the school, the borough council, and the governors were working in cahoots with the Employment Tribunal, because soon after these hearings, they concocted allegations against him that he was lying and fabricating complaints. For that reason, he would be dismissed.

Mr Fox showed the author further evidence of discrimination. Official school records show that his qualifications were not recognised **(See appendix).** The school's Self-Evaluation Form (SEF), which was prepared for an inspection, also showed that the head teacher had refused to recognise his qualifications. The table below shows members of staff in the department in which Mr Fox worked. The reader's attention is once again drawn to the column on experience. His teaching experience is recorded consistently as four years, meaning that the head teacher's argument was that Mr Fox was employed without the necessary qualifications. Mr Fox sighed and said in a hoarse voice, 'This is a scandal that needs investigating.' The ET either ignored this evidence of discrimination or simply dismissed it in his face. The ET also turned a blind eye to new contracts which were created to mislead the judge (the same judge) that Mr Fox's contract had been changed. The judge ignored forged signatures in some of the documents which were presented to the tribunal. In short, the judge instinctively protected the head teacher.

Both the name of the department and teachers' initials are fictitious.

Table of Staff teaching music at Grey School

Name	Responsibilities	QTS	Gender	Experience	Current service
SQQQ	Head of Music	Y	F	35	19
C HHH	Second in Music	Y	F	12	11
Mr Fox	**Teacher of Music**	**Y**	**M**	**4**	**3**
PBD	Teacher of Music	Y	M	4	3
LMZ	Teacher of Music	Y	M	4	2

| LKKM | Teacher of Music | Y | F | 16 | 11 |
| KWNO | Teacher of Music | Y | M | 10 | 4 |

Experience = length of time in teaching, current service = time in this school; note: some columns were edited to anonymise the location of this school

The Mr Fox was visibly shaking as he showed me the table above. The reader will notice once again that Mr Fox's initial teacher training was disregarded or ignored. Mr Fox was asking me questions which I could not answer. Why was Mrs. Crow rejecting hard and concrete facts? As he asked that question, he showed me his high school certificates. He retorted, 'My O and A levels were certificated by the University of Cambridge International Examinations, certificates 1980 and 1982 respectively. My teaching qualifications are from the University of Colourbar, a former affiliate of London University. Mrs. Crow had paid £3,525 to an agency so that she could employ me.'

After making reference to his qualifications and where he obtained them, Mr Fox informed me that overseas-trained teachers are viewed as worthless and therefore can be exploited to save some money. The author could not agree with him more. It is not an overstatement to argue that there is a slave mentality among some head teachers in the United Kingdom.

Mr Fox kept on saying, 'My life is ruined.' It was four years after his dismissal, and he had not got a job since then because he was blacklisted. Mr Fox went on to say that when he realised that the head teacher was openly racially discriminatory, he appealed to the governing body. The governors were responsible for coming up with the school salary policy, and it bears their signatures, so they were well-placed to mediate on this issue. The school grievance procedure stipulates that an appeal against a pay decision must be submitted in writing within ten working days of the teacher being notified of the decision. The same salary policy says that the governing body will arrange to hear such appeals within twenty working days of receiving the teacher's written notification to appeal and that appeal decisions will be communicated in writing within twenty-four hours of the decision being made. Mr Fox threw that document to me and said this is a fake document. The author listened attentively to find out what was fake about that document.

Mr Fox said in line with the policy above, he made a formal appeal to the chair of the body of governors through the office of the head teacher. He said he was aware that the governors were responsible for interpreting the teachers' pay and conditions of service and craft their own salary policy. The governors therefore are the custodians of that salary policy. In his appeal, he made an outline of events pointing out what went wrong and the head teacher's response. He said he pointed out to the governors that after passing QTS, the head teacher applied their salary policy inconsistently. He quoted the relevant sections of their salary policy and expressed his displeasure in the manner in which he had been graded. He also exposed the discrepancies that colleagues with the same qualifications as his, from the same institution where he trained and with the same experience as his, had been placed at Main Scale 6 (M6) while he was placed at M3. This scale is equivalent to a newly-qualified teacher (NQT). He highlighted or made an outline of the head teacher's responses too.

Mr Fox said in their very first meeting, she said, 'You still need to complete your QTS. Then we will see your so-called qualifications and experience.' Next, she allayed his fears by assuring him that he had residuals following a 100 per cent pass rate in his year 11 group, who had passed with As and Bs. She had also informed him that she was going to consider these residuals, but she did not say when and when. In their next meeting, she said, 'Your performance is still at "satisfactory", so we cannot grade you to M6.' In yet another meeting, she said the school had no money to pay him. When he made reference to his previous school, pointing out how they correctly interpreted and applied the Teachers' Pay and Conditions of Service, she argued that his previous school had been turned into an academy, and so they could afford to pay their teachers any salary. That claim was obviously not true. When he continued to put pressure, she said, 'After all, we cannot consider your overseas qualifications and experience here.' The author stopped him for a while to find out if the governors were not aware of these developments. Mr Fox's response was that he wanted to make the complaint formal so that he would see the governors' response. He said he had also informed the governors that there was no denying that the head teacher had not only breached a contract but that she also was being discriminatory and racist. She was treating the teacher as an object, with whom she could do whatever she willed. The governors were supposed to see this common sense. As mediators, they were supposed to avert a situation of confrontation. There was no response from the governors for almost a month. Mr Fox informed me that he only realised later that this delay tactic was at the advice of the borough's legal department, to waste time so that by the time the complainant appeals to the Employment Tribunal, the case would be dismissed as out of time. Mr Fox said in his view, the issue of salary could be ruled out of time and not ongoing racial discrimination. The ET did not even want to entertain the issue of racism. The judge was irritated by the topic to the point where he became condescending towards Mr Fox.

Mr Fox wrote another letter to remind the head teacher about the need to work within the time specified in the policy document. Again, there was no response from the governors. He said he felt that either the head teacher was not sending his grievances letters to the governors or the governor simply downplayed his grievances. He contacted the head teacher again, for the third time. He then requested the contact details of the chairman of the body of governors and that of the human resources department. He also informed the head teacher that he was growing anxious about the issue he had raised with the chairman of governors through her office two and half months earlier. He also reminded her of the provisions of their grievance procedure, namely that the governing body will arrange to hear such appeals within twenty working days of receiving the teacher's written notification to appeal. Mr Fox continued to narrate the events of how his complaint was handled by the head teacher and governors. When he reminded Mrs. Crow that thirty days had elapsed since he submitted his appeal, and that he should have received at least an acknowledgement of the receipt of the letter by then, the head teacher said, 'I will forward your letter on to Mr. Morgan as chair of governors, but you can send it to HR yourself, as you are in communication with them. I will reiterate once more that the reasons you state that I gave for your grading are incorrect. I have been through this with you on more than one occasion. I have also explained that the staffs recruited onto higher grades than yourself were employed with recruitment and retention incentives because they entered into shortage subjects, putting them into a different position to you. This all followed the School Teachers' Pay and Conditions document at the time, which we have followed faithfully and to the letter of the law. This obviously not true **(See appendix, Salary Policies)**

The statement above is not true. The reader is referred to the paragraph on recruitment and retention, which contradicted and exposed Mrs. Crow. The reader is reminded that there were eleven teachers recruited in that year. Four of the eleven were deliberately not included in table A above. It would have been difficult to justify why some people were placed at M5–M6 when Mr Fox was placed at M3 and yet had had the same qualifications and experience. So, the discrepancies in table A above should have been avoided if the head teacher had applied the two sections of the salary policy above. It is sad that the head teacher refused to be engaged in respect of the school salary policy. Later on, she openly stated that salary policy did not apply to non-EEA.

Racial discrimination is a very sensitive issue in Britain. Telling me from his experiences, Mr Fox said when a white person discriminates against a black person, instinctively, other whites tend to gang up to protect the offender. Blacks cannot sue a white person over racial discrimination and win the case in court unless he has a good lawyer. That is what happened to him. Mr Fox did not realise that the issue of racism was a very serious one. He realised this when he saw barristers who were hired by the school, the governors, and the legal department of the borough council. Why did they engage a law firm to protect Mrs. Crow? Protect her from what? Were they not sharing the same sentiments towards a black person? Racism is a scourge which will be difficult to eradicate in the United Kingdom because no one is prepared to face it. Whites still look down upon blacks.

Showing frustration on his face, Mr Fox told me that he felt the body of governors were complicit in this case. The chairman of the body of governors (Mr. Morgan) sent him an email inviting me to a discussion to explain the salary policies. Both the head teacher and the governors behaved as if they were dealing with a subhuman person, one who needed to be explained to. Mr Fox continued to tell me that in his response, he politely informed the Mr. Morgan that there might be no need for the meeting which had been scheduled for the following week. He said he reminded the governor that he had appealed to his office because there were mixed messages that he was receiving from the head teacher each time they met. First she was quite clear that she would not recognise his overseas qualifications and experience. On one occasion, she said, 'Complete your QTS, and then we will talk about your so-called qualifications and experience.' Mr Fox said he reminded Mr. Morgan that he was placed at the same grade as one of his colleagues in the department whom he could have taught in high school. He therefore asked him to clarify this point and further stated that in the Luton County Council, there were other OTTs who had obtained this recognition (QTS) and had been placed at M6 depending on their experience, irrespective of where they had received initial teacher training. To assist him, Mr Fox referred to the eleven teachers who had completed QTS the same year as he did. He also reminded him about the provisions provided for in the School Teachers' Salary Policy (2005), quoted above. He reminded Mr. Morgan that the following paragraphs were not applied: paragraph 3 (i) starting salary; paragraph 3 (ii) on experience; and paragraph 4 (i) on experience and 2009 salary policies, both of which are not discriminatory.

Four weeks later, Mr. Morgan, the governor responded **(See appendix).** He started by thanking Mr Fox for the email, in which he asked for a formal response from the governing body rather than a meeting. Mr. Morgan apologised for not responding to him formally in the first instance, stating he felt that this situation was better dealt with by a face-to-face meeting. He went on to say he therefore could confirm how his salary entitlement had been decided in accordance with their policy. 'When you joined Cardinal Newman School, your teaching qualifications and previous teaching experience **had all been gained abroad, and so they are not fully recognised in this country**. You were therefore put on the Unqualified Teacher's Pay Scale. However, due to your previous experience, the head teacher put you at the very top of that scale, which at the time was point 10.' The reader is reminded that the complainant produced evidence of his payslips from his previous school, but Mr. Morgan was not prepared to contradict the head teacher. He was the author of the salary policy. The explanation he tried to provide was not only wrong but confirmed and supported the head teacher, who had already rejected his qualifications on grounds of origin, and both the head teacher and the governor were involved in the short listing and interviews of teachers, including him. Mr Fox said the governor claimed, wrongly, that in his first year of teaching, he attended the necessary course to convert his teaching status to that of qualified teacher, and subsequently, at the end of that year, he was moved from the Unqualified Teachers' Pay Scale onto the Qualified Teachers' Pay Scale, at point M3, in accordance with the Pay and Conditions Guidance document and the Salary Policy. He then made a clearly racist statement. 'You were not entitled to a higher scale, as your previous experience was not in one of the institutions listed in the guidance and policy documents and as your teaching experience had, at the discretion of the head teacher, been taken into account in placing you on scale 10 originally. You will now remain on the Qualified Teachers' Pay Scale until you reach M6, at which time you will be entitled to apply to move through the threshold onto the Upper Pay Scale.'

The reader will see that Mr. Morgan was imposing his authority as the person who had the final say on this matter, so he closed any other possibility of negotiation when he wrote that Mr Fox would remain on the Qualified Teachers' Pay Scale until he reached M6. This level of bullying is unprecedented. There were not qualifications to be converted. That was a racist statement. The reader will notice that Mr. Morgan was not prepared to be engaged in respect of their salary policy. He was rejecting the policy which he himself had authored. The following paragraph 3 (i) starting salary; paragraph 3 (ii) on experience; and paragraph 4 (i) on experience, which he authored, were clear and unequivocal. He declared as a voice of authority when he said, 'You will remain in that grade.' Mr. Morgan, representing the governing body, participated in Mr Fox's interviews with one of the universities in England, when the university was processing Mr Fox's application to enrol for QTS. He therefore knew that Mr Fox's qualifications were equivalent to UK qualifications and were accepted by the university for Mr Fox to be accepted by the university and enrolled for QTS. The author agreed with Mr Fox when he said, 'This is a scandal which should be investigated.' Mr. Morgan went on to make claims which, if investigated, might earn him a jail sentence. He claimed that other schools in the county council might be applying their own pay and conditions policies differently from their school. The reader should know that they are required to follow the guidance set out by the government. Mr. Morgan evaded issues regarding his own salary policy. When he wrote that he could confirm that he was satisfied that the salary policy had been applied to him correctly but declined to comment on other colleagues.

The author shared and sympathised with Mr Fox's dilemma. Mr. Morgan seemed not to be aware that Mr Fox had a copy of the salary policy, which the school had given him when he signed the contract and that he had discussed the issue of salary with Mrs. Crow. Mr Fox asked another rhetorical question: Did Mr. Morgan believe that he was addressing an ignorant person who did not know that there was no school that permitted deviation from the school teachers' pay and conditions documents: 'Guidance on School Teachers' Pay and Conditions'? By the same token, Mr. Morgan was convinced that Mr Fox did not deserve to be paid like his white counterparts.

Mr Fox said in his next correspondence that he had to correct the misinformation in Mr. Morgan's responses. The author realises the amount of frustration Mr Fox was facing. It my view that Mr Fox was reminding Mr. Mrgan things and events he was aware of but had taken the instinctive route of protecting the head teacher. Mr Fox went on as I listened and took notes. He said he reminded Mr. Morgan that when he joined Cardinal Newman School, he had already taught in other schools in the county council, who had already correctly placed him at point 10, pending QTS (£23,331) **(See appendix)**. This should be the practice across the UK, irrespective of one's qualifications background. The head teacher, Mrs. Crow, maintained or retained this grade. When he then completed 'induction' (QTS), the school ignored or abandoned the policy documents which should have guided them in determining the grading system. At this point, Mr Fox pulled out the national policy and pointed out paragraphs 37.1, 18.1a, and 4.2 which seemed to correspond with

'Cardinal Newman School Teachers' Salary Policy (2005)'. I must admit that I was shocked when I learnt that the two documents were a mirror of each other. Mr Fox concluded that when Mr. Morgan, the governor, said, 'You were not entitled to a higher scale, as your previous experience was not in one of the institutions listed in the guidance and policy documents,' he was simply being racist, because both documents do not raise the issue of race or origin of qualifications. Mr Fox said that he reminded Mr. Morgan that the pay guidance did not deliberately isolate his country for eligibility, because his country, Colourbar, was a former colony of the UK. Mr Fox informed him that he reminded Mr. Morgan that he (Mr Fox) trained during the colonial period, which explained why his qualifications were equivalent to the UK qualifications. At this point, Mr Fox showed him a document headed 'National Recognition Information Centre (NARIC)'. The author went through that NARIC certificate and was left with no doubt that the governor, Mr. Morgan, and the head teacher, Mrs. Crow, were simply racists who were bullying an innocent teacher. Mr Fox kept on saying, 'My life is ruined.' He realised that when you challenge authorities about racism, you should be prepared to face the consequences of dismissal and a lifetime ban from teaching in the UK.

Mr Fox challenged the governor by comparing himself with a junior colleague in the department. Mr Fox argued that together we were regarded as newly-qualified teachers. While this is true for him, that he was NQT, Mr Fox said, 'It is not for me.' He went on to go over the information, which, in my view, the governor knew about. 'I did not train in the UK but went through an induction to be recognised as qualified teacher who can practise in the UK (QTS).' Mr Fox then challenged the governor, Mr. Morgan, about a very sensitive issue, which exposed him. He asked him to explain how his salary policy was applied in respect of the twenty-two black and minority ethnic or non-EEA teachers he had employed in the last five years. The table below shows where they obtained initial teacher training. Mr. Morgan brushed this challenge off, for two reasons. First, he could not deny that they had employed twenty-two MBE, most of whom were still in school. More importantly, Mr Fox informed the author that the salary policy had been applied arbitrarily; some benefited, while others lost out but did not dare challenge it **(See table below)**. It is for the latter reason that Mr Fox was sacrificed. He had exposed them in a big way, and they were not prepared for that. Mr Fox intimated to me that he regretted having done this, because head teachers had absolute power, which has enabled them to abuse MBE teachers for years. The unions know it. They have carried out a survey and brought the results to Parliament, but it has always been swept under the carpet. Unions themselves have no power to stop the abuse of people they purport to represent. The names of these teachers were withheld to protect their identity. The author was given access to documents with shocking evidence.

List of BME teachers who trained overseas (OTTs) employed at Cardinal Newman Secondary School.

Name	Year obtained ITT	Country where Initial Qualifications were obtained	Main scale after QTS	Experience at the time of joining GS
SMS	1985	Zimbabwe	M6	19
VJV	1998	Jamaica	M5	9
ROR	1995	Ghana	M5	11
Mr Fox	1985	Zimbabwe	M3	23
WWW	1998	Jamaica	M6	7
BMB	1995	Zimbabwe	M5	9
MSM	1985	Zimbabwe	M6	19
ADA	2003	Nigeria	M3	9
NSN	2005	Zimbabwe	M3	3
HFH	1905	Ghana	M6	10
PMP	1986	Zimbabwe	M6	18
TRT	1993	Pakistan	M6	15
TOT	1999	Nigeria	M6	9
DBD	1999	Ghana	M6	15

EBE	1998	South Africa	M5	16
MMM	1985	Zimbabwe	M6	17
BAB	2005	South Africa	M3	3
GMG	1998	Zimbabwe	M6	20
TST	1998	Ghana	M5	10
RSR	1993	Zimbabwe	M6	18
KGK	2002	South Africa	M6	6
LML	2007	Kenya	M3	1
PBP	2007	Ghana	M3	1
IFI	1989	Zimbabwe	M6	19
ENE	1987	Zimbabwe	M6	21
BJB	1989	Zimbabwe	M6	19

Names of these teachers are withheld for data protection. The evidence of discrimination above could not be wished away. Mr Fox politely expressed all due respect to the office of the governor but still made his point that he felt that there might be a need to revisit and reconcile the policy documents quoted above. In his view, if the governor visited the relevant sections of the salary documents, it was going to persuade him to see that the head teacher was discriminatory in placing him at M3 while his colleagues were placed at M6. He also reminded the governor that he had not failed to interpret these documents properly and further believed that these documents could not be discriminatory.

The author asked Mr Fox whether he had made an attempt to speak to other members of the governing body to find out their views. His response was that there was a breach of the complaints procedure. Mr. Morgan did not respond to issues he raised above. He should have allowed other members of the governing body to intervene, but he did not. As a result, he was in breach of paragraph 20 of the complaints/appeals procedure, which explains very clearly that any complaints with regard to performance pay awards or pay in general, including threshold, should be referred to the head teacher in the first instance. If a teacher's concerns cannot be resolved at this level, a formal appeal may be made to the subcommittee of the governing body set up to deal with such matters. No governor who has been involved in an appellant's pay decision could serve on the appeal committee for that teacher. Mr. Morgan and Mrs. Crow prevented Mr Fox from having access to the whole panel of body of governors. The two bullied him and intimidated him. More evidence below shows that the two had agreed to work out a strategy to dismiss Mr Fox. To do so, they needed some evidence of some documented to cover their back. They turned to Luton Borough Council five years after the initial complaint was submitted. Mr Fox showed me a couple of correspondences he made with some officers in the borough council, dating back four years. The same HR department Mr Fox had been in communication with, but without getting tangible help, convened stage-managed meetings. It is difficult to understand why a group of young ladies were used to sacrifice Mr Fox. Stage-managed hearings were convened. No one was prepared to listen to or look at the documentary evidence of discrimination.

CHAPTER 2

THE COUNCIL COLLUDED IN DISMISSING THE COMPLAINANT

Mr Fox informed the author that he realised that he was naive to place his hopes on the Luton Borough Council, which he knew to be a multinational, multiethnic, multi-faith, and multicultural society. One would expect the administration to be sensitive to or at least conscious of phobias that might run across the community. Ideally, there should not be one ethnic group which is more important than the other. The way his case was handled by Luton Borough Council suggests that the council is at variance with the principle of equality. This chapter exposes LBC's duplicity. The HR played a key role in dismissing the complainant. It was systematic and concerted. By dismissing the teacher assistant of trumped-up charges, they made it a sure case that the teacher was deprived of a possible source of finance to engage solicitors or any form of support whatsoever. The second role of the Luton Borough Council was to then provide legal support. It was well-calculated. Without legal representation, chances of winning his case were reduced to zero. Finally, the legal team would advise Mrs. Crow to (i) ignore the existence of pay policies, (ii) reject documents she authored, (iii) deny statements she had made, and (iv) create new contracts with forged signatures. Mr Fox believes that the borough council could have done something if an EEA teacher had complained about discrimination.

The Role of the Human Resources Department

Mr Fox informed me that when he realised that no investigations were being carried out by the body of governors, he turned to the human resources department in the borough council. The role of the Luton Borough Council will be examined in some more detail in chapter 3 below. The scandals which were committed by the HR, the legal department, and other departments which helped to dismiss Mr Fox should be exposed and the officers investigated. Mr Fox informed the author that he believes the Luton Borough Council was also complicit. Mr Fox had contacted the LBC's human resources department first, making enquiries and seeking advice. After a couple of communications, one of the HR advisers (ATA) informed him that Cardinal Newman School should have a school teachers' pay policy which should conform to national terms and conditions of service, especially the school teachers' pay and conditions document, which are you watching this game? He attached to his email. Mr Fox said after going through this document that he was convinced that the head teacher had a case to answer. Two months later, Mr Fox made an official complaint to the HR department and described his situation in some detail. In the following weeks, Mr Fox made a formal complaint about discrimination and asked for advice. Mr ATA advised that if there was any misinterpretation of any policy or conditions of service, as he had described in his letter, then he must take it up with the school. Following his next correspondence, Mr ATA informed him that the school's salary policy should mirror the school teachers' pay and conditions document, which he sent to him as an attachment. Two weeks later, Mr Fox presented my research findings to the HR department following their advice to investigate whether the school was interpreting and applying the instrument correctly. No one responded to this official letter. A Ms FHF sent him 'Grievance Appeal Form: Appendix Two' which he completed and sent to the director of children and learning, a Mr Bull. The form was intercepted by Ms RSR, the corporate information officer, Complaints Section, at the Luton Borough Council. Ms RSR refused to assist Mr Fox, arguing that council could not consider this complaint under the council corporate complaints procedure, for two reasons: Under section 6 of the procedure (see attached copy), it makes it clear that this policy cannot be used when other actions are being pursued; and if you are not employed by the borough council but by the governing body of Cardinal Newman School, your complaint should be directed to the governing body. Mr Fox informed me that he felt as if he had hit a rock at this point. Mr Fox and I agreed that Ms RS had received information about this issue, but we could not tell whether she was working under instructions to frustrate Mr Fox.

While he was wondering what to do next after being shut out by Ms RSR, who claimed that LBC would not deal with such an issue, Mr Fox received a letter from Ms FHF, claiming to be HR team leader. What struck Mr Fox was that Ms FMF claimed to be ignorant of this case at the beginning. Although Ms RS distanced LBC from interfering in investigating allegations of race discrimination, in a twist of events, both the HR and the legal department of the Luton Borough Council took over this case in a very dramatic but suspicious fashion as events below show. Ms FHF (HR advisor) took over investigations of a case she was already aware of. Making reference to Mr Fox's correspondence, Ms FH said, 'Your letter of 9 August suggests that you may expect the matter of breach of contract to be re-investigated when this has already been subject to the previous investigation by the school and to the scrutiny of the ET which found in the school favour.' The author asked Mr Fox what this lady was coming to investigate if she was not going to investigate a breach of contract. The reader is reminded once again that there were no investigations. It took the complainant three years to exhaust the school-grievance procedure. By the time he turned to the employment tribunal, Mr Fox said his case was three years out of time, so it was dismissed on that basis. Judges did not even bother to examine the issue of discrimination. It is difficult to know the purpose of the meetings Ms FH was instituting, in retrospect, if she was not revisiting the issue of breach of contract and discrimination. The author agreed with Mr Fox's observations that the borough council and the governors had agreed to save the head teacher and sack the complainant on a concocted charge of gross misconduct for taking the school to the employment tribunal. Mr Fox concluded that, after a couple of correspondences with HR, his fate had been sealed already before the following two meetings were held.

Mr Fox received an advance warning in a letter from Ms FHF who claimed to be the team **leader (See appendix).** Ms FH warned that she was aware of his concerns and the comments he made in a grievance letter to HR but would point out that many of the issues raised in his were largely historic and had already been dealt with under the school's grievance process. She therefore did not want to visit them again now. Ms FHF took this stance as team leader and manager of the Luton Borough Council's human resources department. The instructions she gave to her subordinates, the reader will notice below, were to reject any evidence which had to do with breach of contract. The HR team were clearly working on instructions from council lawyers, and the governor (Mr. Morgan) to charge the complainant and dismiss him. This meeting was just a formality. The first hearing by the borough council was conducted soon after the ET hearing. This was three years after the incident had taken place. These meetings were not intended to investigate the issue but to create grounds for a charge. The stage was set by Mr. Gareth Fay, the deputy head teacher, who dropped a bombshell a couple of days before the meeting. Mr. Gareth Fay claimed that during his investigations into Mr Fox's allegations of racial and religious prejudices, he was unable to substantiate the claims he had made. Mr Fox informed the author that he did not know or understand how Mr. Gareth Fay had conducted his investigations without involving the complainant **(See appendix, Gareth Fay).** The claimant's case was summarily dismissed. After Mr. Fay's recommendations above, the HR began with the foundation laid by Mr Giraffe. To make sure Mr Fox understood the purpose of the meetings which the HR had organised, another HR leader and advisor Ms SGS sent an advance warning in which she stated her awareness that Mr Fox had been to an employment tribunal, that the issues had been addressed, and that he had been paid correctly. She concluded, 'I don't wish to go over old issues with you.'**(See appendix).** The reader should notice that Ms SGS was echoing the same sentiments expressed by Ms FHF earlier. If HR was not coming to investigate issues that were at the core of the problem for three years, why had they made arrangements for this meeting?

Drama in the Meeting

Mr Fox showed me minutes of the first meeting held at the council premises. In that meeting, Ms CLC, one of the panellists, a member of HR, dismissed Mr Fox's attempt to present his case. She emphatically said, 'We are not going to get anywhere by looking over your documents at this point.' They were openly rejecting his evidence. Another member of that team, Ms SGS, remarked that staff members concerned were deeply hurt by his accusations. Ms SGS went on to ask, 'Do you see why people no longer want to work with you?' At this remark, the complainant observed that the implications of that statement were that he had already been sacked by some members of staff. The union representative who attended the meeting also observed, 'We have to work with people even if we do not agree with them.'

The third member of the team, Ms CLC, could not hide her emotions. 'We will need to read through the whole document,' she said. The team leader, Ms SG, then dismissed the meeting by saying, 'We need to go away and read these documents properly. We cannot make any decision today.' It was clear that these girls were desperate to go away not even bothering to read anything Mr Fox had presented before them. The union representative expressed concern over what was going on. 'It is interesting how you are concerned about how other people feel, but you have not asked how Mr Fox feels.'

Without repeating the quotes above, it suffices to remind the reader that (i) the team rejected the evidence of discrimination and breach of contract, (ii) they pointed out that other members of staff were no longer prepared to work with the complainant, and (iii) they expressed emotions in support of the head teacher and other members of staff. The verdict was going to come from the governor (Mr. Morgan). There was no feedback from the ladies, as promised. Instead, they arranged another meeting in which the same routine of rejecting Mr Fox's evidence of breach of contract and discrimination. The reader should notice that the ladies on the panel were working under instruction to reject everything Mr Fox said.

Racism in the UK is like a terminal disease with no cure. If the law against racism worked, Mr. Morgan and the three ladies from LBC would have known that they were breaking the law. The other problem is that there is no appetite on the part of authorities to investigate issues of abuse, discrimination, the sacking of teachers, and the creation of an 'offenders register' which results in the lifetime ban of teachers. The saddest part of it is that other head teachers simply check your name on the register; once they find it, they never ask anything but dismiss you immediately. There are pockets of institutions within government departments over which government has no power. The education secretary has no legal power to investigate what is going on in schools. Apparently, this is not the only department which is in chaos.

Mr Fox said after the first meeting above that he expected the inevitable. Mr. Morgan himself was going to flex his muscles and demonstrate once and for all that he was in charge, and anyone who dare challenge his authority would face the consequences. Mr Fox remarked that Mr. Morgan exercised the level of racism and bullying which was last witnessed during the slave-trade era. This case had been dragging on for three years. In that period, the complainant exhausted the grievance procedure and appealed to every office that he thought might help. After the meetings recorded above, his fate was sealed. They could not just dismiss the complainant without the two meetings recorded above. The head teacher, Mrs. Crow, and the governor, Mr. Morgan, were adamant that a non-EEA could not be treated like his white counterparts. This position had not been challenged before. They needed to get rid of me very quickly but in the most unorthodox way. The charge and dismissal was based on the two meetings referred to earlier, where and when the complainant was not allowed to present issues of breach of contract. During these hearings, the panellists worked to instructions like robots, rejecting any and all evidence of breach of contract and racial discrimination. A decision had already been made to charge and dismiss the complainant. Following these fake meetings, the complainant received the correspondence which outlined the charges and dismissal **(See appendix).** The same governor Mr. Morgan wrote a charge letter as outlined below. Mr. Morgan wrote to confirm the outcome of the disciplinary hearing. Mr Fox and I could not agree on the import of the expressions which were used by Mr. Morgan. Was Mr. Morgan suggesting that the ladies had made a decision in that meeting that Mr Fox should be dismissed? What powers did they have of making such decisions? The ladies refused to listen to Mr Fox's account or even to look at the documents which he had brought to the meeting. So how did they arrive at the charges? Be as it may, Mr. Morgan outlined the charges. It was alleged that Mr Fox had committed gross misconduct under section xxiii of the school's disciplinary procedure by making false, inaccurate, and misleading statements; he had also committed gross misconduct under section xxiii of the school's disciplinary procedure by making vexatious, malicious, and/or frivolous complaints.

The reader should notice that Mr. Morgan wrote to confirm the outcome of the disciplinary hearing which he had set up. Mr Fox said these charges were concocted and were unfounded. His crime was that he challenged the school over discrimination and breach of contract (See Cardinal Newman School teachers' salary policy—paragraphs 3 (i), 3 (ii), and 4 (i) above—and school teachers' pay and conditions document 37.1, 'Pay and Conditions Guidance Document and Salary Policy', 18.1.1a and 37.1). In the same charge letter, Mr. Morgan reiterated Mrs. Crow's remarks which expose racism. They wrote that although he (Mr Fox) understands he is an overseas-trained teacher (OTT), in his mind, there is a misunderstanding that although we fully accept his degrees and other qualifications as valid and authenticated by NARIC, we cannot accept the teaching qualifications of those trained outside the EEA. Surely the education secretary cannot afford not to take action when issues of race discrimination, bullying, and dismissal are raised in Parliament. Following the above racist statement, the complainant was dismissed with immediate effect. The reader's attention is drawn to contradictions expressed by the governors. In an appeal hearing, Ms LSL, another lady who was introduced as a member of the governing body, said, 'When you (Mr Fox) presented your case to governors, you focused on the issue of your pay, the school's failure, in your view, to accept your qualifications. The governors did not accept your assertion that you have been racially discriminated against due to the pay point you had been placed upon when you moved to the main scale'. Mr Fox was convinced that the contribution made by Ms LSL above suggests that Mr. Morgan handpicked people who were prepared to protect Mrs. Crow, the head teacher, not professionals. One wonders how schools choose office bearers for such important jobs when they cannot understand the implications of their actions. The author could not agree with him more.

Mr Fox appealed against the allegations which led to his dismissal. Prior to the meeting, he received a correspondence from Mr. Morgan, who wrote to advise that there would be an appeal hearing to consider his appeal against disciplinary action as set out in his letter. 'Please note that the appeal panel can only consider those points in your letter that comply with section 7.1.2 of the disciplinary process,' he wrote. Mr Fox informed me that the focus of hearing had shifted from his grievances to charges against him for challenging the school over practices which had been going on for years. The governor took it upon himself to dismiss Mr Fox, no matter what. He therefore dismissed the issue of breach of contract and discrimination and focused on the charges which he had concocted. In bragging fashion, Mr. Morgan, the governor, wrote again to remind him that, in this country, if you dare raise issues about racial discrimination, no one will listen to you. Mr. Morgan reminded Mr Fox of the obvious: that he had for over five years now been advised by everyone that he had consulted that the decisions taken by the school regarding his salary were correct **(See appendix).** He also pointed out that Mr Fox had exhausted all avenues of appeal that the governors had any jurisdiction over with regard to this matter, and therefore this appeal panel would not consider any further points on this. This is the ugly face of institutionalised racism.

Mr. Morgan showed Mr Fox that he was in charge and no other power would challenge his decision. Indeed, by this time, it was clear that Mr Fox had hit a hard wall. This institution was refusing to acknowledge their documents which Mr Fox was showing me. In empathy, the author found himself shedding tears as Mr Fox was sobbing, saying, 'My experiences were and are still as painful as those of a prisoner on death row when he knows that he has been mistakenly sentenced to death.'

Mr. Morgan kept to his word. He supported the head teacher, Mrs. Crow, even on an issue they both knew was wrong. Mr. Morgan argued that Mrs. Crow was clear and had explained, 'It is your teaching qualifications which are not recognised in this country according to national policies.' This was chilling **(See appendix)**. Mr Fox had informed me earlier that he had been interviewed by both the head teacher and this particular governor. On the basis of his qualifications, he had been offered a teaching post. What had gone wrong? I asked Mr Fox to show me his qualifications and the NARIC certificate, and indeed they were genuine. For me, even to anyone reading the passage above, this is institutional racial discrimination. This is a very sad scenario. This level of racial discrimination is unbelievable. Mr Fox pointed out to me that Mr. Morgan may have been a racist even before this incident. How can someone be employed as a teacher without a teaching qualification? The complainant had been employed on the basis of a qualification which had been obtained overseas. Mr. Morgan was part of the vetting panel when Mr Fox was employed and when he applied to do QTS. He is the one who was tasked to verify his qualifications and his teaching content. For him to confirm that the head teacher, Mrs. Crow, rejected his qualifications because they were obtained overseas is mind-boggling.

Mr Fox lamented why the responsible authorities were not concerned that the education system was being run by people who had such a mindset. He showed me again the correspondences from FMF (the HR leader). The HR leader argued that she did not wish to go over old issues with him, which suggested that the team already had a judgement, which they were ready to present to the bosses. Besides, Ms FMF could not hide the fact that listening to the claimant trying to present evidence of discrimination was wasting their time. She dismissed Mr Fox, saying, 'We are not going to get anywhere by looking over your documents at this point.' They had no interest in analysing documentary evidence and seeking further explanation from the claimant. Ms SGS openly said, 'We need to go away and read these documents properly. We cannot make any decisions today.' Once again, they had no interest in analysing documentary evidence and seeking further explanation from the claimant. They could not hide their emotions, either. That staff members concerned were deeply hurt by his accusations. Mr Fox said that he and his union representative were shocked by the revelations that the complainant had already been dismissed by other workmates when they said, 'That is why people no longer want to work with you.' His union representative objected to that attitude, saying, 'We work with people we don't like in life.' Workmates have no right to dismiss another staff member. Unfortunately, this is what happened.

It is worth noting that SGS, as HR leader, instructed her team to execute her plan of action. To that end, Messrs SGS, CLC, CLH, and FMF spoke with one voice. They worked to instructions from Mr. Morgan. They were to reject any evidence from Mr Fox and frustrate him.

Mr Fox went as far as to say he suspected that these girls who had been handpicked to execute Mr. Morgan and Mrs. Crow's plan had no knowledge of relationships among such concepts as teacher development agency (TDA), NARIC, GTC, and the school. They were not capable of making judgements on issues of such magnitude.

A ray of hope came from one of the panellists, Ms CLC (who was Afro-Caribbean), who seemed to have an idea of the role of NARIC. This lady had been co-opted to colour the composition of the panel. She was surprised why the head teacher could reject the complainant's qualifications. When this lady tried to ask such questions as 'When did you do your training? How were you employed if they said they don't recognise your qualifications? Did you do QTS? What did the university say?' This member of the panel was called outside by Ms SGS for a chat. Mr Fox said he felt that she was being reminded not to contradict their brief by their superior. Mr Fox informed me that he left this meeting without any doubt that this was a missed opportunity to rectify the wrongs they had done.

When one puts together all the remarks referenced above, one is left with no doubt that Black and minority ethnic teachers are regarded as objects which can be disposed of when they are no longer needed. The reader is referred to and reminded about the provisions of Grey school teachers' salary policy. The relevant paragraphs, 3 (i), 3 (ii), and 4 (i) above and the school teachers' pay and conditions document 37.1, 'Pay and Conditions Guidance Document and Salary Policy' 18.1.1a and 37.1, are all clear about how teachers should be remunerated irrespective of the origin of their qualifications when they have been verified **(See appendix, Salary Policies)**. The head teacher applied this instrument arbitrarily. The head teacher and the governors refused to be drawn to the policy document above arguing that the complainant is non-EEA. There was breach of contract in respect of salary. When the complainant made reference to the salary policy, the position of governors was that we cannot accept the teaching qualifications of those trained outside the EEA. What the reader should note is that the complainant was employed on the basis of the same teaching qualifications of those trained outside the EEA, that these qualifications are recognised as equivalent to the UK qualifications, and that he could not have been allowed to do QTS if his teaching qualifications were not recognised in the UK. Mrs. Crow was adamant that we have to write in the experience from the point of view of when you gained QTS in this country, as your previous qualifications were not recognised here. The kind of racial discrimination and bullying the complainant experienced in this school is mind-boggling. Finally, both the head teacher and body of governors could not be drawn into talking about their salary policy. The reason is clear: each of the twenty-two black and ethnic minorities who worked in this school had been treated differently. The head teacher used whim in making life-changing decisions about a black and ethnic minority, and the governors supported her.

As you read this document, the complainant is paying costs to the Luton Borough Council for providing legal representation to the school. Be as it may, it should however be noted and emphasised that, in the period referred to in this chapter, there were three Ghanaians, one Kenyan, one Nigerian, one Indian, two Jamaicans, two South Africans, and twelve Zimbabweans who had been employed by this school. The evidence above shows that the salary policy was not applied faithfully because we are non-EEA. It is doubtful if the head teacher and governors did not know that they were breaking the law. These issues should be investigated and the law should take its course. Mr Fox said he did not think that it would come to this. After this dismissal, the head teacher posted his name on an 'offenders' register which is kept by schools in the region. The department for education should investigate the mistreatment of black and ethnic minority teachers. It should also investigate the fact that the complainant is compensating the school for all expenses incurred to the borough council's legal department. Mr Fox felt that he might not be the only one who had suffered this level of modern-day barbarism and enslavement. By blacklisting him, the head teacher had ruined his teaching career in the UK. They have made it a sure case that any would-be his employer he was a dismissed teacher. This is how cruel institutionalised racism is. The perpetrators make sure that you are destroyed once and for all and are silenced. The reader is once again reminded about a survey which was conducted by unions: In 2017, Runnymede, NASUWT, and

Act for Racial Justice published the report, 'Visible Minorities, Invisible Teachers: BME Teachers in the Education System in England', which presented the NASUWT Big question survey findings, alongside other research, evidencing poor experiences across the school system for BME teachers, with discrimination and unequal treatment starting early in teachers' careers, with lower pay on average than peers, amid a pervasive culture of racism. The unions and activists confirmed institutional racism in the United Kingdom, and yet nothing is being done about it.

The Role of the Legal Department

The next institution which was engaged was the Luton Borough Council's legal department, which was assigned to represent Mrs. Crow in a case of allegations of breach of contract and discrimination which had been taken to the employment tribunal. One would have expected the legal department to handle this case as professionals who knew the legal implications of the statements the head teacher had made. The reader is once again reminded about the documented facts on this issue. This background is important because it exposes the ugly face of institutionalised racism. After completing QTS, the claimant hoped that his salary was going to be adjusted from Unqualified point 10 (£23,331) to Main Scale M6 (£30,148.00), according to the school teachers' salary policy (2005), paragraph 3 (i) starting salary, paragraph 3 (ii) on experience, and paragraph 4 (i) on experience (see the highlighted sections of the policy above). When the complainant was employed by Cardinal Newman Secondary School, his salary was already at point 10 of the Unqualified (£23,331) from his previous school. After completing QTS, the complainant's salary did not change. Mrs. Crow's reasons for not grading the complainant according to the salary policy were made clear in the racist remarks she made. She said, 'You still need to complete your QTS; then we will see your so-called qualifications and experience.'

In the meeting that followed, she said that she was going to consider the residuals of your GCSE As and Bs. 'That is when your salary will be adjusted.' In another meeting, when she was becoming exasperated, she defiantly said, 'What you are getting is the correct salary.' All this time, she was refusing to be drawn to her salary policy. When Mr Fox tried to remind her that she was deviating from the requirements of the national teachers' pay and conditions of service, which other schools were following, she dismissed that by arguing, 'Your former school was turned into an academy. They have more money than us so they can afford to pay their teachers any amount of money.' Mrs. Crow revealed her racist attitude when she categorically stated, 'We cannot consider your overseas qualifications and experience because they are not recognised here.' Mr Fox's qualifications were not accepted in this particular school or institution. When Mr Fox challenged her about the discrepancies and inconsistencies in which she applied her own salary policy, she argued, 'The staffs recruited onto higher grades than yourself were employed with recruitment and retention incentives because they entered into shortage subjects putting them into a different position to you.' This was obviously not true. Remember, Mr. Morgan, representing the governors, had expressed similar racist sentiments by saying, 'When you joined the school, your teaching qualifications and previous teaching experience had all been gained abroad and are not fully recognised in this country.' This was racial discrimination. He had categorically said, 'You were not entitled to a higher scale, as your previous experience was not in one of the institutions listed in the guidance and policy documents.' Both the head teacher and the governor had made discriminatory statements which were prosecutable.

The legal team analysed all the communications and realised that Mrs. Crow had a case to answer. In 2007-2008, civil servants had received a 2.5 per cent salary increase from which Mr Fox benefited. His salary was raised from £23,331 to M3 (£24,048) because of the 2.5 per cent increase. If his salary had been calculated and assessed according to 3 (i), 3 (ii), and 4 (i) of the salary policy above, his salary should have been at point M6 (£30, 148). By 31 July 2012, he had been prejudiced of £17,000.00+/-. It is sad to point out that Mrs. Crow, Mr. Morgan, and the legal team were aware of these facts. The defence team admitted race discrimination was at issue at the ET hearing. In a witness statement, the defence team wrote that the learned judge found one complaint of discrimination on the grounds of race. That is the allegation of direct discrimination in less favourable treatment by placing the claimant on point M3 of the pay scale for classroom teachers. This admission at the time was important in that it solves the debate about whether or not the claimant was racially discriminated against. Mr Fox felt that Luton Borough Council missed an opportunity to reprimand Mrs. Crow for making open racial remarks as a head of such a big school. Indeed, the council would have demonstrated zero tolerance to racially-motivated discrimination, bullying, and intimidation. Instead, they chose to dismiss the complainant for challenging such attitudes.

The lawyers of the school made desperate measures to get rid of Mr Fox. They made offers to settle the matter but dictated the terms **(See appendix).** BME teachers are not covered in the rights of teachers in the United Kingdom. The sad thing was that Mr Fox's union representative watched helplessly as the teacher was being abused. By making this offer as transcribed above, the lawyer was overriding the contract which Mr Fox had signed at the time of accepting the contract. These are the signs of institutionalised racism.

Mr Fox informed me that the same unreasonable offer was made three times. The termination date was moved each time the offer was made. The third and final offer was made when Mr Fox had tried to engage a solicitor whom he was not able to pay. The solicitor had made some discussions with LBC legal department. Mr Fox informed me that the legal department was not prepared to negotiate with him. They continued to dictate terms and conditions of his termination. They said the school was prepared to make the offer to him again and give him a lump sum payment equivalent to three months' pay (after tax/NI), payable within twenty-one days of the completion of a COT3 agreement. He would be given a reference. They would waiver the costs award that was made against him in the previous employment tribunal claim. They demanded that this offer would need to be accepted within the next five days, as after that time he would have to start drafting a defence and there would be no scope for settlement after then. They also demanded that as part of the agreement, he would have to sign a confidentiality clause and agree that he would settle all and any claims he had, whether in the tribunal or county (or any other) court.

An examination of these offers shows a master-servant relationship. The Luton Borough Council was aware that they were dealing with a complex issue of race discrimination, so they wanted to terminate the contract by dictating terms. Because they were dealing with an inferior non-EEA person whom they regarded as having no human rights, they dictated the pace and course of events. When the offer did not yield the desired result, they turned to creating new contracts. The first task of the legal team of Luton Borough Council was to pressure the complainant to release all the documents in his possession. The next step was to craft a new contract which would discharge the complainant from work on (See new contracts and offer letters). These documents are available for scrutiny. The dilemma of the legal team was that they did not know if Mr Fox had a statement of particulars and if so which one. They created three offer letters in retrospect, four appointment declarations, and four statements of particulars which were in response to Mr Fox's allegations of breach of contract and racial discrimination. These 'new contracts' were presented to the employment tribunal, but the latter never queried why a contract

The Ugly Face of Institutional Racism

would change for a single person in the public service. This institution (employment tribunal) also gave a blind eye to glaring irregularities which should have been challenged. Mr Fox says he protested at the ET that all the signatures in these new contracts were forged, but again, the judge ignored him.

The table below constitutes the original contract which Mr Fox signed on 05 June 2007. On the day of signing the contract, he received a staff handbook which had very important policy documents as indicated below.

The Table of the Original Contract

Dates	Documents	Comment
05/06/07	Offer Letter	Signed by the head teacher
05/06/07	Acceptance letter	Signed by the teacher
	Policy documents received	
	School Teachers' Salary Policy (2005)	Staff Handbook
	Statement of Particulars	Staff Handbook
No date	Grievance Procedure	Staff handbook
No date	Code of conduct	Staff handbook
No date	Race Equality Policy	Staff handbook

When Mr Fox turned down the offer of a settlement of £17, 000.00, **(See appendix, Without prejudice)**, they resorted to changing the contract. They produced documents which were purpoted to constitute the New Contract, and four appointment declarations with Mr Fox's forged signatures. This was a dirt game obviously master minded by their lawyers.

Attempts to create new offer letters thereby changing the original contract (See appendix)

DATES	Documents	Comment
27/06/07	Another offer letter	Signed by Mrs. Crow
21/08/07	Another offer letter	Signed by Mrs. Crow
10/09/08	Another offer letter	Signed by Mrs. Crow

This argument was accepted by the Employment Tribunal. The ET connived with the school to save the head teacher. There was also a set of Appointment declarations which had forged signatures purported to have been signed by Mr Fox.

Table of appointment declarations purportedly signed by Mr Fox

Date	Document	Comment
25/06/07	Appointment declaration	Forged signature
25/06/07	Appointment declaration	Forged signature
18/10/07	Appointment declaration	Forged signature
13/10/08	Appointment declaration	Forged signature

(See appendix)

If the reader goes back to the first document, they would be reminded that the head teacher paid £3525 for Mr Fox **'to become a permanent member of staff.'** This level of desperation defines 'institutional racism'. Mr Fox pointed to the contradictions among these nine (documents) and asked which one was authentic. He asked the obvious questions:

* Why were so many documents created and in retrospect?
* Why do we have forged signatures in two of them which had the same date?

- How were they reconciling these documents with the first one which employed him on permanent basis? Mr Fox informed me that they had no clear answer. He observed that the Judge upheld those documents and argued that he was to blame for signing, even when he protested. This scenario shows that Mrs. Crow has a case to answer. The legal department misleads the employment tribunal by falsely giving the wrong picture that the contract had been changed and Mr Fox had consented.

Statements of Particulars (See appendix)

To reinforce their argument that the contract had been changed with the consent of Mr Fox, school served Mr Fox with five dofferent Statements of Particulars all of which had conflicting information. The first statement of particulars **had no date.** This is the standard statement he received when he signed the contract. The reader will notice that it has no dates. Besides, the next paragraph pertains to the Criminal Records Bureau and Check (Disclosure); followed by Induction Programme; and Place and Type of Work. The paragraph on Salary does not mention a figure. It does not have a termination of contract date, because he had been employed full time. The next four statements of particulars attempted to (i) fix the date of the contract, (ii) specify salary figure, and (iii) suggest when and how the Luton Borough Council was going to discharge him from duty.

The Second Statement of Particulars (See appendix)

What has been inserted in this second documents includes: dated, Grade: Unqualified, the claim that he was deamed to be in continuous employment with the school, his contract of employment is fixed, the reason is due to your Unqualified Teacher status in the UK, and the date of termination of the contract. Finally he was prepared that, the employment of Overseas Teachers is temporary for up to four years while you secure qualified teacher status and will be reviewed at that time subject to the staffing needs of the school and them continuing to hold a valid work permit. Lastly his salary was calculated and fully assessed at Point 10 (£22,764 per annum) in accordance with the relevant School Teachers' Pay and Conditions Document and will be reviewed annually. The advisor did not realize that Mr Fox's salary already at Point 10 (23,331) due to the 2.5 per cent increment in 2007.

The Third Statement of Particulars (See appendix)

Focus on the next one was on the period of employment. This one had the same dates. The terms of employment was limiting his contract of employment to 'fixed term due to your Unqualified Teacher status in the UK and the expiry of my visa'. This information was false and inaccurate. Once again he was made aware of the date when his employment with the Council would be discharged. His salary was wrongly quoted at Point 10 (£22,764).

The Fourth Statement of Particulars (See appendix)

Focus of this Statement was the reason for discharging him, '**employment was fixed term due to the expiry date of your work permit** and, the date when the Council would discharge him. On Salary: Again his salary was not at Point 10 (£22, 764 per annum) but at £23,331.

The Fifth Statement of Particulars does not have period of employment. It begins in a very unusual way: 'If you are made redundant, periods of your service with other employers may be aggregated with your service with the school for purposes of calculating your redundancy payment in accordance with the redundancy payment (local government) (Modification) Order 1983, as amended. This Statement was designed 3 years after his claim of discrimination had been raised. At this point they realized that they had to match his current salary with the Statement of particulars. His salary was indeed at Point M3 (£24, 048).

Analysis of the Statements of Particulars

Each one of the five statements was intended to mislead the judges. There were three pieces of vital information to which the judges were directed. The first set of information was the date of commencement, which was 05/06/2007. Second was the statement, referred to as 'Continuous Employment with the School', which had a specific date. These new documents were created with the view to limit Mr Fox's contract of employment to a fixed term so that the council would discharge him on specified dates. **Strangely, the reasons for fixing his term of employment tended to be speculative and therefore differed from one statement to another.** For example, the reasons for terminating Mr Fox's employment would be due to his unqualified teacher status in the UK, while in the next one, it was due to unqualified teacher status in the UK and the expiry of his visa. In the next one still, it was fixed term due to the expiry date of his work permit, and in the final one, it said, 'If you are made redundant, periods of your service with other employers may be aggregated with your service with the school.' The last statement's purpose was to inform the complainant of his fate, namely that he was going to be made redundant. Finally, the salary was pegged at £22,764. The reader will notice that this figure was wrong. Mr Fox's salary was already at £23,331. The lawyers and the judges had skilfully removed the focus of Mr Fox's grievances from breach of contract and racially-motivated discrimination. These statements were therefore created to address the new grievances which had been created at the prehearing sessions. The school's argument shifted from breach of contract and race discrimination to 'a contract which was honoured to the letter'. This is a huge scandal for which Mrs. Crow should be investigated and charged.

Mrs. Crow was advised to dismiss Mr Fox without compensation so that he would not be able to hire a law firm to represent him. This strategy had a double effect. On the one hand, without a representative, Mr Fox was not able to convince the ET that the legal team had crafted a new contract as indicated above. More significantly, the ET was not convinced either that the statements made by the respondent above were racist. The head teacher openly said 'You are not EEA, we do not recognise your qualifications here; you do not qualify to be paid like an EEA because of your country which is not in the EEA'.

The judges instinctively supported the offender. Mr Fox informed me that he was naive to believe in the justice system. The case was dismissed with costs. The head teacher, Mrs. Crow, and the governor, Mr. Morgan, were adamant that a non-EEA could not be treated like his white counterparts (see chapter 1). This position of discrimination had not been challenged before. They needed to get rid of Mr Fox very quickly but in the most unorthodox way. The charge and dismissal were based on the two meetings referred to earlier where and when the complainant was not allowed to present issues of breach of contract. In a strongly-worded letter to the ET, the legal team had already outlined the reasons for pending dismissal; the claims are scandalous, vexatious, and unreasonable **(See appendix, Trumped up charges)**. They threatened him with costs to recover the Luton Borough Council's expenses. Then Mr. Morgan wrote to confirm the outcome of the disciplinary hearing which he had set up. These charges were concocted and were unfounded. Mr. Morgan wrote to confirm the outcome of the Disciplinary Hearing that Mr Fox had committed gross misconduct under section xxiii of the school's disciplinary procedure by making false, inaccurate, and misleading statements and that he had committed gross misconduct under section xxiii of the school's disciplinary procedure by making vexatious, malicious, and or frivolous complaints. Racism is institutional and difficult to eradicate. The Judge was clearly on the side of the headteacher. Mr Fox intimated to me that the Judge would on many occasions fail to hide his attitude, condescending, ignoring pertinent questions which were not addressed.

Mr Fox crime's was that he had challenged the school over discrimination and breach of contract (see Cardinal Newman School salary policy paragraphs 3 (i), 3 (ii), and 4 (i) above and school teachers' pay and conditions document 37.1, 'Pay and Conditions Guidance Document and Salary Policy' 18.1.1a and 37.1). In the same charge letter, Mrs. Crow further stated, 'Although he (complainant) understands he is an Overseas Trained Teacher (OTT), in his mind there is a misunderstanding that although we fully accept his degrees and other qualifications, as valid and authenticated by NARIC, we cannot accept the teaching qualifications of those trained outside the EEA. **'(See appendix Governors' letters)**. Following the above racist statement, the complainant was dismissed with immediate effect. Mr Fox's case was dismissed, and he was asked to pay £17,000.00 in legal costs to the Borough Council. This is the ugly face of racism.

Pressure from the Borough Council's Legal Department to Sell Our House

While Mr Fox was struggling to get a job because of the circumstances outlined above, the Borough Council was enforcing charging orders on family property for the debt incurred while he was trying to stand up for his employment rights. The Borough Council provided legal services to protect a head teacher who believes that BME are second-class citizens who do not deserve to be paid as their counterpart members of the EEA. The reader is reminded that the legal department made offers of settlement. Mr Fox informed me that the relationship between the school (as represented by their solicitors) was that of a servant and master. They were aware that there was a contract but were overriding that contract and then demanded a mutually-agreed termination of Mr Fox's employment. The first offer was made on 31 July 2012. The second offer was made on 14 November 2012. The third and final offer was made through someone who had offered to assist Mr Fox. **(See appendix, Without prejudice)**.

A close analysis of these offers says a lot about that Master –Servant relationship referred above. By this date when the offers were made, Mr Fox was **owed** £17,090.50 **in salary arears** because he had been paid on the wrong pay scale which was his claim to the Employment Tribunal **(See appendix, paragraph 5.1d)**. At the same time, Mr Fox was servicing a **debt of £17,894.78** in Employment Tribunal costs. Simple mathematics show that the solicitors had worked out that, if Mr Fox had accepted the offer, it would be adjusted to pay off the debt accrued in ET costs. The terms offered in that termination offer were as follows:

* gross **(owed £17,090.50 in salary arears)**, to be made payable within twenty-one days of the termination date.
* Mr Fox would be given a clean reference if he agreed.
* Mrs. Crow was going to set aside the disciplinary proceedings.
* In return, council would not enforce the costs order of £5k.
* Agreed clean reference (which was not guaranteed)
* Mr Fox would drop all cases (claims) pending in the ET or County Court.

They threatened Mr Fox that this matter was now at the enforcement stage with the county court and that it was likely that the council (the Luton Borough Council) might shortly seek a charging order on his property for the debt or apply for an attachment-of-earnings order. Mr Fox would also need to agree not to pursue any claims (including those for personal injury) against the school in the future, and he would need to withdraw his grievance and any appeal to the employment appeals tribunal.

Indeed, the Borough Council applied and were granted a charging order on Mr. Fox's property. At the time of compiling this manuscript, Mr Fox was servicing a debt of £17,894.78, which he owes Luton Council and which is being monitored very closely by one of the lawyers.

As the Luton Borough Council mounted more and more pressure for Mr Fox to pay more towards his debt, Mr Fox wrote them to remind them of his circumstances and to also plead with them that they persuade Mrs. Crow to provide a reference to his agencies so that he would be able to work and pay their debt. Mr Fox wrote to Mr Duck **(One of the solicitors)** proposing to pay £10 towards the debt of £2,320 because of his circumstances. Mr Fox reminded Mr Duck that he was already servicing another debt by the same which he was struggling to pay. Mr Fox provided evidence of post-dismissal victimisation to the council and that he was unemployable. In his response, Mr Duck acknowledged receipt of Mr Fox's application but requested more detail on his income (current benefits, family income) and expenditure (all credit card/loan balances, current repayment terms), before he could fully consider his offer. Mr Duck requested further details about the debt management charity who had taken over Mr Fox's financial problems. Mr Duck requested a resubmitting of these details. He also asked Mr Fox to send details and schedule of income and expenditure and how he paid his mortgage. Mr Fox showed evidence that he was doing part-time care work and was given a job-seeker allowance. Mr Fox said he could not believe that in this country he could experience a life of a slave. He felt the world crumbling on him. He had knocked on almost every door, looking for someone to come to his rescue, but none did. He had exhausted the school grievance procedure, but no one had listened to him.

Mr Fox intimated to me that the reason he was sharing his ordeal was to expose scandals of this nature which go unnoticed because powerful people who are supposed to protect the weak and the downtrodden are actually exploiting them instead. The Borough Council was supposed to investigate discrimination. Instead, they provided lawyers to protect Mrs. Crow, who abused the teacher (see chapter 1, 'Breach of Contract', and chapter 2, 'The Role of the Luton Borough Council'). Besides the abuses, they threatened to make him homeless when at the same time they were refusing him a reference to work. At his weakest point, when they knew that he would not be employed, the Luton Borough Council's legal department put more and more pressure as they enforced an order of recovering costs awarded to them by the ET.

Mr Duck wrote a letter that sent chilling sensations through Mr Fox's whole body. This is a council that is supposed to provide services to its people, whose services include accommodation, but it continued to pile pressure on an individual whom they racially abused. When Mr Fox was struggling to make ends meet, he received an email from Mr Duck. He informed Mr Fox that he had been advised by Cardinal Newman School, that he he continued to fail to make payment of his monthly instalment of £160 per month, **he had been instructed to make an application to enforce the sale of his property without further notice.** This is a whole mark of institutional racism. The Council was pursuing and monitoring the recovery of this debt for two reasons. They needed to recover costs incurred when they represented Mrs. Crow in the ET. However, in the process, they wanted to bury Mr Fox for good so that he would never speak again. They were threatening to sell the property to recover £17,000. They had imposed this situation on Mr Fox. Both Mrs. Crow and the Council acted inhumanly. Mr Fox did not refuse to pay, but he could not pay because they made him unemployable. Mr Fox wished these two institutions would be investigated for racism. Mr Fox's situation is unusual in that he is compensating the institution which should have protected his rights. The HR and the legal department were supposed to advise the head teacher accordingly and resolve this dispute over salary. In Mr Fox's case, they did not because they were also benefitting from underpaying Mr Fox.

CHAPTER 3

LUTON BOROUGH COUNCIL AND THE EMPLOYMENT TRIBUNAL WORKED IN CAHOOTS

In a case of discrimination, disclosure plays a central role. When Mr Fox was dismissed he was alerged to have made false, inaccurate or misleading statements or vexatious, malicious, and/or frivolous complaints (of racially motivated discrimination) **(See appendix, Trumped up charges).** Mr Fox's argument to the ET was that he had evidence that the school had employed up to 21 teachers or more from overseas (Non-EEA) **(See table below).** Mr. Fox had argued that he had raised the complaint that he had not been been paid like his counterparts and the reasons he was given by the head teacher Mrs Jane Crow, chair of governors Mr Andy Morgan, and the vice chair of governors Ms Linda Scuder respectively were shocking **(See appendix, discriminatory statements).** By any standards, these sentiments were racist to say the least. The school refused to disclose the details of these Non-EEA teachers. The ET judges looked away on this scandal. The court orders were ignored. (See table on page

The Ugly Face of Institutional Racism

List of BME teachers who trained overseas (OTTs) employed at Cardinal Newman Secondary School (Transcribed).

Name	Year obtained ITT	Country where Initial Qualifications were obtained	Main scale after QTS	Experience at the time of joining CNS for Cardinal Newman School
SMS	1985	Zimbabwe	M6	19
VJV	1998	Jamaica	M5	9
ROR	1995	Ghana	M5	11
Mr Fox	1985	Zimbabwe	M3	23
WWW	1998	Jamaica	M6	7
BMB	1995	Zimbabwe	M5	9
MSM	1985	Zimbabwe	M6	19
ADA	2003	Nigeria	M3	9
NSN	2005	Zimbabwe	M3	3
HFH	1905	Ghana	M6	10
PMP	1986	Zimbabwe	M6	18
TRT	1993	Pakistan	M6	15
TOT	1999	Nigeria	M6	9
DBD	1999	Ghana	M6	15
EBE	1998	South Africa	M5	16
MMM	1985	Zimbabwe	M6	17
BAB	2005	South Africa	M3	3
GMG	1998	Zimbabwe	M6	20
TST	1998	Ghana	M5	10
RSR	1993	Zimbabwe	M6	18
KGK	2002	South Africa	M6	6
LML	2007	Kenya	M3	1
PBP	2007	Ghana	M3	1
IFI	1989	Zimbabwe	M6	19
ENE	1987	Zimbabwe	M6	21
BJB	1989	Zimbabwe	M6	19

Pre-hearing Reviews (PHR) or Case Management Discussions (CMD) (See appendix)

Mr Fox made several applications to the ET for disclosure. Mr Fox informed me that the responses from the ET were frustrating to say the least. The ET and the school organised Pre-hearing Reviews (PHR) or Case Management Discussion (CMD) which resulted in the changing of the original claim he had submitted to the ET. The CMD scheduled for 9March 2012 was **to identify and resolve any outstanding issues. The only outstanding issue was disclosure.** The one scheduled for 21 June 2013 was for the **respondent to strike out or for a deposit order on the grounds that the case has no or little prospects of success.** Mr Fox sent two other correspondences (16 August and 23 August 2013), requesting the ET to force the school to disclose names above. On 23 August the ET's response was that **the issues can be raised at the out set of the hearing.** The hearing was supposedly converned to see the evidence that Mr Fox was not the only OTTs or Non EEA in school. Mr Fox intimated to me that it was becoming clear that the ET was on the side of the head teacher. When Mr Fox put more pressure on the ET to force the respondent to disclose the list of NON-EEA teachers above, the ET was not kind to him. On 01 October 2013 they exposed their hyposcrisy, **'The Tribunal does not try cases in correspondences. A preliminary hearing will be open and I will consider striking out either party for non compliance'.** Another PHR was arranged for 11 October 2013. The purpose was to clarify any outstanding issues. Mr Fox said as it turned out, the judge did not entertain the issue of disclosure.

Mr Fox's contention was that there were inconsistencies in the manner in which BME colleagues were treated, in comparison to non-BME colleagues. Such evidence, he said, therefore would justify his allegations of racially-motivated discrimination and which resulted in his dismissal.

Mr Fox raised fears during the pre-hearing conferences over and over that the school would be allowed to dictate the pace and direction of events in the ET by refusing to disclose incriminating evidence. The position taken in this book is not to question decisions made by the ET. Mr Fox paused and said, 'I noticed the true nature of human instinct at this ET. Some of the Judges instinctively found themselves sympathising with the head teacher and in some instances could not hide their emotions for they were condescending in the manner in which they responded to me.' He said it was strange that rules and procedures of the ET were flouted by the school lawyers but the judges did not do or say anything about it. The respondent deliberately refused to disclose the information requested (**see table above**). They also demonstrated that they did not respect the orders of the employment tribunals. An examination of the table above exposes Mrs. Crow and Mr. Morgan. The table of BME teachers has nineteen BME teachers, each one of whom was treated differently. That same list exposes inconsistencies in the treatment of BME on the grounds that they are non-Europeans (sentiments expressed above). Qualifications and experience were taken into consideration for the majority of OTT on completing QTS. The list shows that some of the OTTs were paid in accordance with the current salary policy referred to above while others were not. The issue of qualifications was not raised for any one of them because OTT qualifications are verified by NARIC and by the relevant authorities at the point of signing the contract and at the point of enrolling for QTS with the Teacher Development Agency (TDA). The only difference between the complainant and the rest of the non-EEA is that the school had paid £3,525 to buy the complainant, so they were not prepared to pay more. Does this not remind us of the slave error? Once a slave had been sold, he or she lost all their rights and assumed those bestowed on him by the new master. The complainant would like to submit that this was a case of exploitative contract for non-Europeans. The issue of qualifications could not be raised in respect of one teacher when the school employed nineteen teachers with the same background as that of the complainant. Mrs. Crow also misled the ET that those who were placed at M6 were in specialist subjects. That is not true. There were a couple of other teachers who were in the same department as the complainant, who were placed at M6 when they completed QTS. She also misled the ET that she had not accepted some qualifications from non-EEA members. The judges could not challenge the head teacher as to why she had employed someone whose qualifications they did not recognise. Once again, this is not true. The complainant had teaching qualifications rated by NARIC as equivalent or similar to UK qualifications **(See appendix).** Mr Fox requested the ET to consider striking out the defence of the lawyers on the grounds that they had crucial information which they adamantly refused to disclose, but they did not do so. Each of the following case management orders instructed the defendant (the school) to disclose non-EEA or BME who had trained overseas (OTT). Mr Fox said the threat that non-compliance to ET orders was summary conviction and the £1,000 fine appeared to have been selectively applied and so was not followed through by the ET. Mrs. Crow was challenged by Mr. Fox at the tribunal to produce a salary policy which they apply to non-EEA, and she openly admitted at the ET that there was none. Mr Fox looked at the judge, hoping that he was going to challenge the head teacher on this very crucial issue, but he did not. Once again, Mrs. Crow has a case to answer. The ET tended to be punitive in the manner in which they awarded costs. Apparently, it was the same judge. In total, £17,000 was awarded to the offender.

As the reader will see, the judge turned a blind eye to crucial information. There was a breach of the case management order with regard to disclosure. Secondly, admitting to the ET that she did not have a separate salary policy for BME, the head teacher was exposing her own inconsistencies in the award of salary to Non-EEA. By dismissing this case when there were those two factors cited above, the judge too was racist.

This justifies the title of the book: The Ugly Face of Institutionalised Racism.

Mr Fox concluded that being White in the UK is a privilege and being Black was a curse. The borough council's legal department refused to comply with rules and procedures of a court of law but nothing happened to them. The ET judges overlooked crucial episodes which could have been used to charge Mrs. Crow. Mr Fox informed me that he sent several reminders to the respondent to comply with ET orders on the issue of disclosure. The legal department rejected that demand in a strongly-worded letter, in which they pointed out that the defendant would not and indeed could not (due to data-protection reasons) supply the information requested. The information in the table above was at the centre of the hearing at the ET. The head teacher, Mrs. Crow, had rejected the qualifications of Mr Fox, arguing that they were not accepted in the United Kingdom. She also remained mute over salary discrepancies which affected BME teachers in the table above. This was incriminating evidence, so they refused to disclose it. The judge ignored that important opportunity to enforce tribunal orders. The reader is reminded that the allegations against Mrs. Crow, the cause for which the complainant went to the ET were that she refused to pay the claimant according to the school salary policy, claiming that she did not accept some qualifications and experience from non-EEA members. These are the same qualifications on the basis upon which the claimant had been employed. Mr Fox looked at me, expressing a degree of helplessness. The documented evidence I was shown by Mr Fox was so overwhelming that Mrs. Crow should be made to answer. Meanwhile, the judge did not see the need for the respondent to disclose information relating to OTT (non-EEA or BME) the school employed in the period referred to. The complainant has the same qualifications as the rest of the OTT in the list above. The case was dismissed, and the respondent was rewarded with costs. The tribunal judge protected the perpetrator of crime.' This is truly the ugly face of institutional racism.

The outcome of Pre-hearing Reviews (PHR) or Case Management Discussion (CMD)

When Mr Fox and I examined the outcome of the so called PHRs and CMDs we both agreed that the ET was working to dismiss Mr Fox's case. These sessions were instigated by the ET and or the Respondent. Each time Mr Fox raised the issue of disclosure, the response was that such issues and any outstanding issues would be addressed at the PHR or CMD. The following issues came out of the so called PHR or CMD:

* The original claim of **racially motivated discrimination** salary areas were changed to **'unlawful deductions of wages' (See appendix, paragraph 5.1b and d)**. This was well calculated. The claim of unlawful deductions was very easy to dismiss.
* The issue of disclosure was not entertained by the judges. In actual fact, they were condescending and sometimes raising their voices in frustration over Mr Fox's insistence that the case could not be heard without disclosure.
* All the documentary evidence of race discrimination were ignored, so were the salary policies. If these three sets of documents had been accepted by the ET, they would never have dismissed this case.

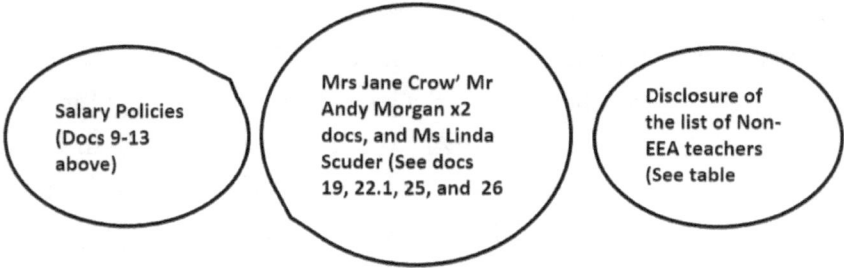

The United Kingdom has a problem of racism in almost every department, unfortunately practised by the most senior professionals. The outcome of the CMD is pathetic to say the least **(See appendix**. Just as the judgement made on this case, CMD was misleading, incorrect, making no reference to the evidence above. Paragraph 3 gives the wrong information when the salary policy were right in front of him. He dismissed the main issue of salary in half a sentence and then dwells on induction. Paragraph is wrong. The judge plays dump by implying that the qualified teacher with seven university (7) degrees was making a claim about a salary policy for OTTs. Mr Fox again showed me that this judge worked to prope up the defence of the school by looking away from the evidence. Paragraphs 7 and 8 make a mockery of the judiciary system. Compare those two paragraphs with ET1 paragraph 5.1 b and d. The judge changed Mr Fox's claim in that claim form. Paragraph 9 of that document seems to be ignorant of the correspondences between parties which were raised with the ET and the latter saying the issue of disclosure would be delt with at the out set of the hearing. When one examines how Mr Fox was treated by the Employment Tribunal, it is difficult to believe that the judges did not know what they were doing. The head teacher, the governors were asked questions they could not answer and each time, Mr Fox drew the attention of the judge to the documents above. The judge still proceded to dismiss the case of racism. The United Kingdom has entrenched Institutional Racism.

CHAPTER 4

BREACH OF THE STATUTORY GUIDANCE ON INDUCTION OF NEWLY-QUALIFIED TEACHERS IN ENGLAND

There was silence for a couple of minutes, and then Mr Fox resumed. Mr Fox asked a rhetorical question again: 'Do you know that slave mentality exists among some head teachers in this country?' As if he was regretting, he continued, 'When Mrs. Crow informed me that she had paid an agency £3,525 recruitment fees for me to become a permanent member of staff, I did not realise that I had sold my rights.' Mr Fox informed me that he was not involved in the financial settlement between the agency and the school. He only realised later that the two (the agency and the school) had agreed that he was going to be treated as a newly qualified teacher (NQT). He was in the dark when he signed the contract on 05/06/07. This is where racial discrimination and slave labour is reflected. The author felt that the head teacher had manipulated Mr Fox's situation. He said the school had employed him on the basis that he was an overseas-trained teacher with qualifications which are equivalent to UK qualifications, but these qualifications were later rejected so that he would be treated as an NQT. When he had settled in the school, he enrolled for qualified-teacher status (QTS). After thorough checks of his qualifications and rigorous interviews which involved the University of

Hertfordshire and the board of governors, the university was satisfied of his suitability, and so they admitted him on a route to **attaining QTS with exemption from induction but with training and support (See appendix, Hertford Regional Partnership)**. The Statutory Guidance on Induction of Newly Qualified Teachers stipulates that because of the route he took as an overseas-trained teacher (from outside the EEA) with twenty years' experience, he would not do an induction once he had obtained QTS and had been simultaneously assessed as meeting the QTS and Core standards by the Training and Development Agency (TDA). See the prescribed form, which has been transcribed as it is (bold for emphasis appears in the actual form). The original below is faint. Once again, Mrs Jane Crow breached another statutory instrument on Induction.

Hertfordshire Regional Partnership (HRP) Accredited Provider

PROFESSIONAL ATTRIBUTES	QTS	CORE
Relationships with learners and young people (Q1, Q2, / C1, C2	Yes	Yes
Frameworks (Q3a, b, /C3	Yes	Yes
Communicating and working with others (Q4, Q5, Q6/C4, C5, C6	Yes	Yes
Personal and Professional development (Q7a &b, Q8, Q9/C7, C8, C9	Yes	Yes
PROFESSIONAL KNOWLEDGE AND UNDERSTANDING	QTS	CORE
Teaching and Learning (Q10/C10	Yes	Yes
Assessment and Monitoring (Q11, Q12,Q13/C11,Q12,Q13)	Yes	Yes
Subjects and Curriculum (Q14, Q15, /C14, C15)	Yes	Yes
Literacy and numeracy and ICT (Q16, Q17/ C17 **(To complete Skills Test**		
Achievement and diversity (Q18, Q19, Q19/C18, C19, C20, C21)	Yes	
Health and well-being (Q21a &b, /C22, C23, C24, C25)	Yes	

PROFESSIONAL SKILLS	QTS	CORE
Planning (22, Q23, Q24/C26, C27, C28)	Yes	Yes
Teaching (Q25a, b, c, d, / C29a, b, c, d, e, C30)	Yes	Yes
Assessing, monitoring and giving feedback (Q26, 27,28//C31,32,33,34)	Yes	Yes
Reviewing teaching and learning (Q29/C35, C36)	Yes	Yes
Learning environment (Q30, Q31/C37, C38, C39)	Yes	Yes
Team working and collaboration (Q32, Q33/C40, C41)	Yes	Yes

The school was given a copy of this report, which showed that Mr Fox was being assessed against both QTS and core standards and was passing. They were also aware of the requirements of the 'Statutory Guidance of Induction of Newly-Qualified Teachers in England'. They knew that the teacher had passed. Why did they insist that Mr Fox should do an induction? What were their motives? Mr Fox remarked that he was treated like a slave who had no rights. The reader is reminded of the requirements of statutes in place which govern induction.

Statutory Guidance on Induction of Newly Qualified Teachers in England says (**1.8**) Statutory induction is the bridge between initial teacher training and a career in teaching. It combines a personalised programme of development, support and professional dialogue, with monitoring and an assessment of performance against the core standards.

(**1.22**) Annex B provides information on those **categories of qualified teachers who are exempt from the requirement to satisfactorily complete an induction period in order to be employed as a teacher** in a relevant school. Paragraph 18 reads: '**An Overseas Trained Teacher (OTT), from outside the EEA, who has gained QTS and was simultaneously and successfully assessed against the core standards and QTS standards**'. It further exempts, 'An overseas-trained teacher (from outside the EEA) with at least two years' experience, who has obtained QTS and who has been simultaneously assessed as meeting the QTS and Core standards by the Training and Development Agency (TDA)'.

The reader should keep in mind the requirements of this legislation. A second visit by the TDA: On 04/06/08, he was observed and assessed teaching two lessons at two different key stages (KS3 and KS4) and passed both QTS and Core standards. Feedback was provided on the GRTP lessons observation form (LOF). The tutor from the university and Mrs KS were both impressed to the point where the latter requested Mr Fox to assist another NQT, by the name of Mr PGP. Mr Fox passed both QTS and core skills.

The statutory instrument was clear that Mr Fox was not required to go through an induction. The school could not manipulate his fate while the university was still in charge. Ms COC from the University of Hertfordshire was impressed by Mr Fox's level of organisation and the quality of lesson plans and his teaching. After observing him, she scheduled their feedback for after school. When they met for feedback, she remarked that she had had a long conversation with the school coordinator, who recommended that Mr Fox be failed. She inquired with him if there was something wrong. He told her that he was equally in the dark. Ms COC could not fail him because of three factors. First, the end of programme report, which the school had submitted, was full of praise (see below). Secondly, he was meeting all the QTS and Core standards and had submitted enough evidence required for the programme **(See appendix)**. He had performed very well in the three lessons he had delivered. Besides, the coordinator could not provide reasons why they were deciding to fail the candidate. Mr Fox raised a complaint with the TDA coordinator **(See appendix, Correspondence with the University)**. The following Monday, the university responded. The coordinator sent another email reminding me about Skills Tests and reminded Mr Fox that the school was still to send the End of Programme Report.

Mrs. Crow, Mrs KSK, and their advisers were desperate to take control of Mr Fox's destiny. The school had hatched a plan. The only way controlling Mr Fox's destiny was for them to fail him in an induction, that way they would have justification to place him at NQT pay point (M3). Their initial plan was to deliberately miss the deadline for the submission of the End of Programme Report. After a couple of reminders from the university and a bit of pressure from Mr Fox, KSK finally submitted the report below. When they insisted, refusing to sign the final papers, Ms COC gave in to their demands, but as a compromise, they agreed that Mr Fox should do an induction. The report shows that he met both QTS and Core standards, although they decided to acknowledge QTS standards only.

HERTFORDSHIRE REGIONAL PARTNERSHIP: OVERSEAS TRAINED TEACHER PROGRAMME. END OF PROGRAMME REPORT			
Teacher:	Mr	Fox	Absence: None
Mentor:	Sr	YPY	School: Cardinal Newman School
This should be completed and returned to CRP before the date of the final Assessment and a copy made available to a Visiting Tutor from the University of Hertfordshire at the time of the Final Assessment Visit. The teacher concerned should also retain a copy for his/her Portfolio of Evidence			

Instructions: To be completed by the Teacher Mentor or Professional Mentor. Where possible the content should be negotiated and agreed with the teacher. This is a summative report and must include a judgement of the standard of performance achieved in each area of competence. The headings are the areas of competence identified in the Professional Standards for Teachers. Please make specific reference to the Standards which apply (QTS & Core/Induction).

(i) Professional Attributes: Mr Fox has demonstrated clear and high expectations to all students. (Q1,Q2,). These are made explicit to students, who are treated with respect and courtesy. Mr Fox promotes a keen interest in students as individuals, allowing for productive relations to be made. He is involved in Mentoring members of his tutor group. (Q4). He has made a valuable contribution with his Year 8 tutor group to raising money for charity in the School Sponsored Walk. He has made a contribution to the whole school Parental Consultation Day where he showed he could communicate with parents. (Q4, Q5, Q3a, b). He attends all Departmental and Year Team meetings and often makes contributions. (Q6). From meetings with his mentor and the Professional Tutor he acts on advice and feedback to improve his practice. (Q8, Q9).

(ii) Professional knowledge and understanding: Mr Fox has a good depth of knowledge about RE and applies it to Key Stage 3, Key Stage 4 and Key Stage 5 Music Curriculum. (Q14, Q15). He has developed strategies for dealing with any behaviour issues in his classes and has been applying the school's Classroom Management policy (Q10). He teaches a Year10 GCSE Music class and is familiar with the assessment requirements relating to public exams. (Q11). He skilfully makes a regular use of ICT and applies it relevantly to the work in hand (Q17). Mr Fox has made a valued contributions to Year 8 tutor team and is responsible for the delivery of of PSHE to these students. This is a task he has risen to and enjoys good relationships with his tutees. He appropriately seeks advice from his HoY (Q21a, b, Q22). In observations of his lessons he has collaborated with teaching assistants in his classes who support students with their individual learning needs. (Q20) as well as collaborating with colleagues who support our students where English is an additional language (Q19). Mr Fox has attended the in school NQT Induction Programme.

(iii) Professional Skills: Mr Fox is making good progress in this area. His lessons are planned and prepared, making use of suitable resources with all his classes. He sets appropriate objectives for all his students and pays attention to students with SEN or G&T requirements (Q22, Q23, Q24, Q25a, b, c and d). He works well as a member of a large department, contributing to department initiatives and planning (Q32, Q33). He makes use of school and department assessment and recording strategies and in particular he is aware of and makes use of assessment learning strategies (Q26a, b, Q27, Q28). Mr Fox has developed strategies for dealing with behaviour issues (Q30). He regularly contacts parents (Q4,Q5). He is fully involved in reporting to parents and has been involved in parents' evenings as well as meeting individual parents when required (Q27, Q28). Mr Fox has given his time and contributed to the Junior School Retreat Programme which is a joint RE/Chaplaincy initiative working with our feeder Primaries (15).

> **Overall comments**
>
> Mr Fox has shown progress during his time with us at Grey School. He has a questioning mind and is always keen to understand how all the 'little things' fit together to make him more effective. He is reflective of his own practice and makes use of this to inform his future teaching. He has developed very good relationships with both staff and students and has become a valued member of the Music department and the Year 8 Pastoral Team. Ms YPY his mentor is pleased with the progress he is making.

Recommendations of the School

The Standards for Qualified Teacher Status have/have not been met. **(Have been met)**

The Core (Induction) Standards have/have not been met.

Please delete as appropriate

N/B: The teacher was entered for either **QTS or QTS with Exemption from Induction** at the start of their OTT programme. The Final Assessment will be made on that basis. **The second level of assessment can neither be added nor removed at this final stage.**

> Signed: YPY (Teacher Mentor), Mr Fox (Teacher), KSK (Professional Mentor) and Head teacher Date: 18/06/08

Please return a copy before the Final Assessment date to:

P L, GTP/OTT Senior Tutor, School of Education, University of Hertfordshire.

As Mr Fox was going through the end-of-programme form above, the author could see contradictions and defiance. Contradictions abounded

The Ugly Face of Institutional Racism

in the requirements of the programme and the recommendations they made. The section on recommendations of the school was left incomplete. They could not delete the recommendation whether Mr Fox had passed the core (induction) standards or not. This is a clear indication that they knew what they were doing.

Recommendations of the School

The Standards for Qualified Teacher Status **have**/have not **been met.**	**They ticked**
The Core (Induction) Standards have/have not been met.	**It was left unticked**

Please delete as appropriate

A comparison of these two documents shows that Mr Fox had passed QTS without the need for an induction

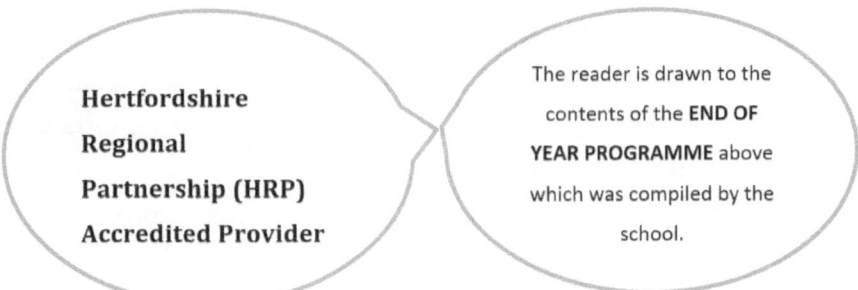

The head of department made a good recommendation **(See appendix, page 2 Head of department's letter)** supporting Mr Fox. Mr Fox felt that the responsible authority had turned a blind eye to the exploitation of BME teachers. Black and minority ethnic teachers are treated like second-class citizens but expected to work the hardest. They have no rights. If they try to exercise their rights, they are dismissed from work with no compensation. Unions are not helping either, because either they are powerless or they have no appetite to help BME teachers. The author examined key documents which were used by the university to track Mr Fox's progress. First, the 'Statutory Guide on the Induction of Newly-Qualified Teachers' clearly states that experienced overseas-trained teachers are exempted from an induction. Mrs. Crow ignored this government instrument and forced Mr Fox alone to do that induction. This was not done out of ignorance. She wantonly broke a statute put in place by an act of Parliament. Mrs. Crow was going to use this opportunity to fail Mr Fox while he was on induction and then dismiss him. This kind of bullying is mind-boggling. BME teachers have no security and have no rights. These institutions can do what they like with overseas-trained teachers.

The author also examined the 'Training Plan for Overseas Trained Teachers Revised for Use with the New Professional Standards for Teachers (See above). This was a contract between Mr Fox and the University of Hertfordshire. The latter knew that there should be no external influence to change this contract. Again, it is clear that Mr Fox was passed both QTS and Core standards by the University. This ruled out the prospects of an induction. The head teacher once again ignored that contract and forced Mr Fox to do an Induction.

When racism is institutionalised, the offender is protected at the cost of human life. Mr Fox was sacrificed because he dared challenge institutionalal racism. The author has already hinted above that when one White person breaks the law relating to racism, other institutions instinctively support the offender and sacrifice the victim of racism. This is the Ugly Face of Institutionalal Racism in the United Kingdom. In Mr Fox's case, when it became clear that the head teacher, Mrs. Crow, had broken the law about racism, the governors, the council's HR, the legal department, and the office of the director of children services supported the head teacher (the offender) and destroyed Mr Fox's life because he was black and in the minority. It is a sad scenario.

The author also examined the Hertfordshire Regional Partnership: Overseas-Trained Teacher Programme End of Programme Report, which was submitted by Cardinal Newman school to the university. The report also shows that Mr Fox had passed both QTS and core standards. The head teacher, the school coordinator, and head of department signed to agree that Mr Fox had passed the two sets of standards. In a show of defiance, they insisted that Mr Fox should go on an induction. They took over the process from the university, ignoring all the positive recommendations to issue a pass. The university became helpless and gave up. The sad thing is that by recommending an induction, the head of department was contradicting her report to the university (see the report of a competent teacher above). Finally, correspondences from the co-ordinator of the programme at the university assured Mr Fox that no one had the power to change the contract they had agreed on, but the head teacher of Cardinal Newman School, Mrs. Crow was defiant. This is the ugly face of institutionalised racism in the UK.

Although documents analysed above showed that Mr Fox had passed QTS, he was targeted to do an induction. When he raised this issue to the employment tribunal, in an attempt to argue against the allegations of targeted discrimination and bullying, the school produced a list of teachers who joined the school the same time as the complainant. This list helps to define the nature of racial discrimination displayed by Mrs. Crow. Mr Fox had argued to the employment tribunal that he had been targeted for an induction because of his race among the eleven teachers who joined the school in that year. It is not clear what they mean in column D below. Mr Fox assumed that it means they did their QTS at Cardinal Newman. It should not be understood to mean Initial Teacher Training.

List of teachers who completed QTS at CNS in 2008

A	B	C	D	F	G
Name	**Initial teacher training**	Date of QTS	Trained at CNS	Ethnic	**Required to do an Induction by the schol**
1	00/00/00	Jul 00	YES	WB	No
2	00/00/00	Jul 00	Yes	WB	No
3	00/00/00	Jul 00	Yes	WB	No
4	00/00/00	Jul 00	YES	WB	No
5	00/00/00	Jul 00	YES	WB	No
6 Mr Fox	**31/12/1985**	**Jul 2008**	**YES**	**BME**	**Yes**
7	00/00/00	Jul 00	YES	WB	No
8	00/00/00	Jul 00	YES	AB	No
9	00/00/00	Jul 00	YES	WB	No
10	00/00/00	Jul 00	YES	WB	No
11	00/00/00	Jul 00	YES	WB	No

It was disheartening that, when the head teacher presented these figures which show that among the eleven teachers who completed QTS in that year, the ET judge did not support Mr Fox when he asked why he alone was forced to do an induction. The important data to take note of in table D is that the head teacher is arguing that Mr Fox completed his initial teacher training on 16/06/2008 and yet Mr Fox had completed Initial Teacher Training, twenty years earlier than the year when he enrolled for qualified teacher status in the United Kingdom. The record above suggests that Mr Fox was trained at Cardinal Newman School. This is absurd, because 16/06/2008 is the year when he completed QTS. In that regard, Mrs. Crow's argument was that Mr Fox was employed without a qualification. The fact of racially motivated discrimination cannot be disputed. A close examination shows that there is one BME on this list. Column B suggests that Mr Fox obtained Initial Teacher Training (ITT) in this school in 16/06/2008, when he joined the school. Mr Fox was employed on the basis of his overseas ITT, which he obtained in 1985. The head teacher goes on to suggest in column C that Mr Fox became qualified in 2008, the year when he completed QTS, which means she was rejecting his ITT. Again, the head teacher would not have employed an unqualified teacher. Column F shows that he is the only BME in that group, and in column G, he is the only one who was forced to do an induction. By that date, the complainant had been teaching for twenty-two years. Why did the head teacher reject his ITT? Why did she break the law and force Mr Fox to do an induction? The answer is simple Mrs. Crow wanted to find an easy way of dismissing the teacher by failing him in the induction because he had challenged her act of racial discrimination.

Mr Fox shared with me his chilling experiences. The head teacher, Mrs. Crow, insisted that Mr Fox should repeat a course he had completed and passed. He read to me sections of the 'Statutory Guidance on Induction of Newly-Qualified Teachers'. The reader is reminded about the purpose of induction according to the statutory instrument:

> (1.8) Statutory induction is the bridge between initial teacher training and a career in teaching. It combines a personalised programme of development, support and professional dialogue, with monitoring and an assessment of performance against the core standards.

When Mr Fox enquired from the coordinator what the purpose of this induction was, her reply was **'to tie up the little, small, minute bits'**. Indeed, the school could not come up with meaningful induction targets. Induction targets below made a mockery of the whole induction exercise.

INDUCTION TARGETS	COMMENTS
(i) to be able to juggle with duties;	A whole of induction to juggle with duties?
(ii) to further understand KS 4 RE syllabus;	Professional knowledge and understanding: Q14, 15. Also refer to the Head of Department's recommendations
(iii) to develop further classroom management strategies with control and consistency;	This contradicts the report
(iv) to develop the role & responsibilities of a tutor; and	See Professional Attributes (Q1, Q2,).
(v) to be proficient in teaching Critical Thinking.	This would contradict their report.

This is the highest level of cruelty.

After taking over from TDA (illegally though), the school was working to destroy Mr Fox's teaching career.

The reader is reminded that the Mr Fox had been assessed for QTS against the core standards and had passed. Also, the school had recommended in a report submitted to the TDA that the complainant was doing well. Throughout the induction period, he did not see where any one of these targets were visited or even referred to. In my honest opinion, this induction had nothing to do with developing any skill because it was assessment after assessment. **This was an opportunity to manipulate Mr Fox's fate.** He raised the issue of racial discrimination, harassment, and bullying in an email to TDA on, but the latter had lost the mandate when they allowed Mrs. Crow to breach a contract between TDA and Mr Fox. He no longer had anywhere to turn to when things were going really bad. He complained that the process of conducting induction was turning unprofessional and was going to damage his image, destroy his ego, and demoralise him. For Mrs. Crow, the induction was premeditated and calculated. Mrs. Crow was beginning to create evidence of a teacher who was failing an induction so that she would meet the requirement of section 6.1 of the 'Statutory Guide on Induction of Newly-Qualified Teachers in England' (paragraph 2.108), section 6.2, 'School Teachers' Salary Policy (0000) (paragraph 4(i) and 6(iii) 'School Teachers' Pay and Conditions Document' (0000) (paragraph 18.1.6), **which authorise the school to discharge the teacher or withhold some points on grounds of underperformance.**

Strategy 1 Mrs Jane Crow hired a Ms Val Girling from outside the school who walked into Mr Fox's classroom unannounced and informed him that she had been hired by the school. Ms VGV was disappointed when he informed her that he had passed QTS the day before. She felt bad that Mrs FMF had misled her into believing that she was coming to supervise a QTS who was failing. The reader is reminded of desperate move by Mrs. Crow to gather as much evidence of a failing NQT as she could.

Strategy 2 Senior Teachers were tasked to just walk in Mr Fox's lessons unannounced and observe his lessons.

Summary of Lessons Observed. Copies of the 19 lesson feedback available for inspection.

Month and year	No of observations	Dates
June 0000	2	00/06/00; 00/06/00
September 0000	2	00/10/00; 00/10/00
November 0000	1	00/11/00
February 0000	1	00/02/00
March 0000	3 including joint	00/03/00; 00/03/00; 00/03/00
April 0000	1	00/04/00
May 0000	2 including joint	00/05/00; 00/05/00
June 0000	4 including joint	00/06/00; 00/06/00; 00/06/00; 00/06/00
Total	16 + 3 witnesses	19 observations

This scenario is illegal by any standards. Bullying, intimidation, and verbal insults were perpetrated against the teacher, sometimes in front of students which is against the National Policy on Induction. Mr Fox was not aware of the targets, and the visits were impromptu. He also pointed out that Mrs FMF (deputy head) organised the first visit of the induction to take place on the second day after he passed his QTS. The arrangements for this induction had been made before the final assessment. In that regard, the school was in breach of paragraph 1.20 of the statutory instrument. It is also worth noting that unless a teacher has an identified problem, the teacher cannot be observed every month, and some times he was observed three times.

Strategy 3 When the school felt that they had gathered adequate evidence to recommend a failing candidate to Luton Borough Council, they invited the coordinator secretly to validate their judgement that Mr Fox was failing induction. Mrs. Crow was aware of and supervising the execution of the plan to get rid of Mr Fox. The meeting was expected to endorse the consensus decision by Mrs KSK, Ms YPY, FMF, and Mrs. Crow that Mr Fox was failing. Mr JM held two separate meetings, one between JM, YP, and KS, and another between JM and Mr Fox. Mr JMJ outlined Mr Fox's possible fate, namely that he had the powers to (i) endorse the school's decision to fail him, in which case he was not going to teach in England the rest of his life, or (ii) overturn that decision and pass him, (iii) or give him the opportunity to repeat. This was the harshest and most turbulent period of Mr Fox's life. He said he felt the highest level of injustice, indignity, dehumanisation, degrading, and humiliation.

The minutes of the meeting he had with SLT were entitled 'For the Assessment of NQTs Who Are Experiencing Problems'. The school had contacted Council to inform them that they had an NQT who was failing. Mr Fox was not made aware of this situation. After observing his lesson, Mr JMN was puzzled. He could not confirm that Mr Fox was a failing teacher. He enquired with him if there was a problem. Even as he tried to explain to him that the school had suddenly turned vicious against him, he still could not understand why, especially when I was doing so well. The school's obsession with building evidence against a failing teacher resulted in ignoring the requirements of the 'Statutory Guide on the Induction of Newly-Qualified Teachers in England'. The number of lesson observations trebled, and many of them were impromptu. The Council sent another person by the name Mr JBJ on and convened two meetings again, but one set of minutes were produced. Mr JBJ discovered that there was (i) **no programme for this induction**, and he recommended that there should be one. (ii) Mr JMN also noted that **there was no training support in place** (Mrs KSK admitted to Mr JBJ in the minutes of the meeting they held that no support had been arranged until they invited Council to validate a failing). (iii) A programme was hastily crafted after this visit. In this new programme, they focused on behaviour management (C4) of a registration group that he met for fifteen minutes in the morning. The reader is reminded that the TDA, Ms YPY, and the end of programme had certified that he was doing very well in that standard (C4. The head of year was using that group to undermine his authority. The head teacher enlisted the support of Senior Management Team (SLT) to execute her plan. The SLT was instructed to observe as many lessons as they could and judge lessons as weak or mediocre . This exercise of creating evidence was conducted meticulously. All lesson observations were rated as weak. Joint lesson observations were put in place so that one of the people observing becomes a witness. Mr Fox told the author that the school had made recommendations to fail him when they did not know what they were doing. The process of Induction was influenced and dictated by the desire to fail the teacher (victimisation) so that he would be dismissed from the job which to him constitutes racial discrimination. This is clear evidence of harassment, victimisation and intimidation. Besides, Mr. Fox had a full teaching load plus other duties in school. The NQT coordinator supervised and checked on him every Wednesday while he was on break duty. Once again, a close examination of lesson feedback shows that he was doing quite well.

The whole idea behind the amount of coordinated pressure was to force Mr Fox to resign on his own. The organisation did not inform Mr Fox or draw his attention to the statutory instrument which was to govern the most important phase of his life. Enshrined in this instrument were/are: (i) the reasons for induction (paragraph1.8), (ii) my responsibilities (paragraphs 1.16), (iii) my rights (paragraph 2.70 page 109), (iv) complaints procedures (paragraph 2.82), and (v) consequences of failing the programme (paragraph 2.108). The situation outlined above is illegal and should be investigated. There was no time in his teaching career in this school when he was rude to the head or anyone for that matter. Mrs. Crow must have agreed with the agency that Mr Fox was to be paid as a newly-qualified teacher so that she would recover the money she had paid them. The degree and level of determination to destroy his life cannot be explained.

Strategy 4 The other four SLT were each given a task as hit men. Once again, their ferocity towards Mr Fox cannot be explained unless they were remunerated in one way or the other. They instituted joint observations. There was evidence that KSK was determined to fail him. One thing which became clear was the strategy of conducting joint observations, in which I could see people liaising/discussing/conniving and therefore agreeing that the lesson was not going on well. First was the HoD with FMF, then KSK with the HoD, then the HoD with JTJ, an assistant head teacher. These other people had been dragged in as witnesses to confirm that Mr Fox was failing. On his first assignment, Mr JTJ appeared to be professional. After observing the first lesson, he requested another lesson to observe, because what he had witnessed in the lesson he had observed, with Ms YPY, contradicted what he had been made to understand. In fact, when these two disagreed (Ms YPY and Mr JTJ), the former retorted, 'So, am I going to change my crit?' Was she expecting JTJ to endorse the position the school had agreed on? When the two observed another lesson the following week, JTJ categorically said he had nothing more to discuss with him. He was happy. In effect, JTJ was so impressed with my ICT presentation that he proposed that he be given an opportunity to make one presentation during 'Craft of the Classroom' sessions. This was not to be, lest it contradict the position of the school that he was a failing teacher. Mrs KSK, too, requested me to mentor an NQT by the name PGP.

As I listened to Mr Fox relating his ordeal, I felt that indeed BME teachers are treated as objects in United Kingdom. The paragraph above prove beyond doubt that SLT treated him that way because, when they forced him to repeat a course he had passed, he had been stripped of all human rights. This is the ugly face of institutionalized racism. All the members of senior leadership team did not see anything wrong in treating a member of staff the way they treated Mr Fox. In fact, this bullying was normal in the eyes of these teachers. These are the evils of racism. The reader is reminded once again that, when all this was happening, students saw it happen, and a few asked why that was happening.

Strategy 5 The author allowed Mr Fox to continue. He observed that 'Another strategy Mrs. KSK employed to frustrate me was to assign other teachers who had direct contact with me to fail me. The head of year 9 (HoY9) was the handiest one, because he supervised registration every morning (see the role of HoY below). What stressed me most was that word was spreading around that I had failed the course and that I was going. Some of my year 9 tutees would come to me with tears in their eyes, asking me why I was going away. Although I felt humiliated, I could not share my problems with the students who sympathised with me. Meanwhile, Mrs KSK's feedback throughout 0000 reflected contradictions and or confusion. The descriptors outlined how well lessons were delivered in terms that show outstanding teaching, but these descriptors contradicted the final grade. What became clear in the observation critiques/feedback was that instead of acknowledging the teacher's role in the good lessons, KSK praised learners for learning well. The teacher's role was removed from the scene altogether.' At one point, KSK made an admission that I was doing well:

You are finally doing it our way. This is England; people who trained in England take up to five years to complete QTS, so there is no way you can complete yours in such a short space of time. It took five years for my husband to be employed in this school.

The problem with these remarks is that KSK was convinced that I could not complete QTS in one year and that I could not do any better than teachers who trained in the UK. This again reflects her attitude towards me. Did I need to know the status of her husband? KS was failing me because I am not British, and not being British connotes inferiority. I felt these statements had racial overtones. When I reported racial abuse to the HoY9, KSK ignored it.

Strategy 6 Another feature which cropped up in the induction period was that new targets kept on coming up. The HoY9 was deliberately undermining my authority in my tutor group. That tutor group became more and more difficult to handle. In the groups that I taught RE, there was not even a single incident of behaviour management. Behaviour management with this tutor group became our induction target (C4). Mr JPJ and Mrs KS were fighting a battle I could not understand (see HoY9 below). KSK began to grade me either as 'satisfactory' or 'satisfactory with good elements', and towards the end of induction period, I was graded as 'unsatisfactory'. I could feel the whole Christian world had turned against me. I could not bear the amount of stress that I experienced. I was like a prisoner who had been wrongly convicted and was awaiting execution. I kept praying, but God did not seem to come to my rescue soon enough. After KSK's two observations (KS: 00/10/00, KSI: 00/11/00), Mr Fox informed the author that his health gave in to pressure, and on 00 January 0000, he collapsed in class. Mr Fox had serious heart palpitations. When students went to inform the head of department, she came in and asked if Mr Fox would like to go home. There was no sympathy from anyone in the school. Mr Fox drove home and was admitted the same evening for observations.

Strategy 7 The highest level of frustration which caused stress and high blood pressure came from the HoY9, Mr JPJ, whom he was in contact with every morning. He informed KSW of the problems he was encountering with this particular HoY. He undermined Mr Fox at all cost. All communications were given to students. Mr Fox could not use the assertive discipline system. If and when he did, students would bolt out of the room to report him to Mr JPJ, the head of year. The HoY would come with these students and sit them down. Students would remark in my face, 'We told you. You are not important. The HoY is.' JPJ taunted me day in day out. 'You have to deserve to be respected by students; you are pathetic,' he said. When he tried to make a contribution during a year team meeting, he would ignore me. When he requested that one or two students in my tutor be moved, as was happening in other tutor groups, he brushed me aside and said, 'A white lady is coming to take over that year group.' It became clear to me that he resented me as someone different from him. He observed a PSHE lesson which he was going to fail me. During the feedback he received on that particular lesson (which came four weeks later), his first remark was that he should have consulted him about this lesson. He then went on to condemn the whole lesson.

Mr Fox asked the author to transcribed these terrible verbal attacks on him as they are. He remarked, **'I do not want to be an accomplice in your failing QTS.'** Where was this coming from? When we disagreed over issues of facts, he remarked again, **'In any case, you need to change your accent. Your accent is bad and different, and therefore you need to change it. The other day, when you were reading prayer, it was monotonous. My wife had to change her accent for her to be accepted in the UK'** . Hang on, where was this coming from? These remarks had nothing to do with the lesson he had observed. He had nothing to contribute about that lesson, so he thought of a direct attack. Every morning, Mr Fox dreaded facing that group and the HoY. Meanwhile, this group became the induction target of his supervision on behaviour management. The school 'rewarded' this HoY by allowing him to drop Mr Fox from working with this tutor group or any other. Mr Fox was then required 'to report to another teacher to support him on a daily basis' (this was mental torture). There was surveillance on him every morning. Students would come and inquire why he was going away. Students were indeed very sad because they could not understand why he was leaving the school. Mr Fox said he did not know how much more of his life in school was shared with students. He informed me that he already knew from students that 'a certain white lady' was taking over the group. It turned out to be true.

Strategy 8 Mrs FMF, in her capacity as deputy head teacher, was also assigned to provided evidence on a day-to-day basis. Mr Fox's first encounter with FMF was in 2007, when she was part of a panel that interviewed him for the post of a music teacher. During feedback after the interview, FMF said that although he had done well in the interviews, he could not be offered this post because he was not Christian. From that date, Mr Fox was in contact with FMF on many occasions, since she was the link person to the Music department. When Mr Fox felt he had problems with his classes, he would invite her in her capacity as link person and deputy head. On one occasion, he invited her to one of his year 11 class to observe him and support me because he needed support with that class, which he had inherited from someone. At the end of that lesson, the DH remarked, addressing students, 'You have to sympathise with Mr Fox. You know where he comes from; there is poverty, hunger and strife. So please sympathise with him.' The following day, this class was taunting him using those same remarks. He went to her office to inform her of what had happened. She panicked and wanted to know which particular student had done that. While this was an isolated incident, he was troubled. Where on earth were these remarks coming from? Did students need to know that he was coming from a failed state? FMF felt that he was humiliated in front of children. The next incident, which convinced Mr Fox that FMF had/has an attitude, was when she came to observe . Her judgement on teaching and learning was, 'A satisfactory lesson with definite signs that you are adjusting to our way of doing things! Not easy.' He saw these remarks as positive, an acknowledgment as early as 2007 that he had adjusted (conformed) to her expectations. The dark side of those remarks is that they isolated me as a foreigner ('our way of doing things'). Mrs FMF started clandestine observations which were made in the name of following certain students, and then feedback would be provided. He began to feel that FMF was up to something. He felt she was building a rapport of evidence. In keeping with the idea of building evidence, she appeared in joint observations with YPY. What was strange about FMF's behaviour was that she would not produce independent feedback. The two would sit side by side liaising, discussing, conniving, and therefore agreeing that the lesson was not going on well. Meanwhile, in other remaining lessons where she observed Mr Fox, was not passed.

The final incident which proved that FMF had an attitude was when there was a crisis in the department. The head of department, Ms YPY, was being pressurized to perform all these tasks against her conscience. She showed signs of confusion. Her health gave in, and she was hospitalised for a long time. The school did not make arrangements for who was responsible or coordinating activities in the department in the absence of YPY. The only senior members in the department were BME. Mrs FMF would come to the department every break time to coordinate activities. When a crisis arose in the department because the head of department (who was running the department single-handedly) was away, FMF (deputy head and link person) convened an emergency department meeting. Mr Fox enquired from FMF why the post of deputy had not been filled in six months after CMC's resignation. FMF shocked me. She openly said, 'Mrs. Crow does not want to appoint anyone now but is waiting for a year until NQTs (pointing to AMA, a white NQT) "bed in".' She further said, 'Mrs. Crow does not want to make a mistake (of appointing a black person?) for which she would regret. There are no right candidates.' These remarks caused a stir in that meeting (see minutes and e-mails). There was a heated debate which divided the department into two, whites on the one side and blacks on the other. In my opinion, whether FMF was conveying Mrs. Crow's low opinion of BME in the department or not, she should not have openly informed the department about administration strategies. Telling someone that the head of school has a low opinion of black people is wrong. It appears FMF abused a position of trust. Mr Fox was informed that she was a representative of the interests of BME staff but used that strategic position to manipulate people to her advantage. Who would suspect a police officer of breaking the law unless caught red-handed? This is the ugly face of institutionalised racism.

Mr Fox digressed a bit and intimated to me that Mrs. Crow did not promote BME. Mr Fox gave a couple of cases where BME teachers were sidelined when there were vacancies, only to be asked to mentor a newly-qualified teacher whom she had promoted.

Mr Fox informed the author that he was disappointed most by the role of Ms YPY (head of department), whose attitude towards him spiralled to the point that she no longer wanted to be in the same room where he was doing his work. Mr Fox informed the author that things came to a head, when, out of excitement, he informed the HoD that he had done very well in the second visit of my QTS and that he had been booked for final assessment. Ms YPY panicked. Her first reaction was, 'Are you sure that is what is going to happen? Did you hear them correctly?' The next thing he remembered is that she hurriedly dashed into her office to phone someone. He could not tell why she had behaved this way and who she was phoning. YPY's attitude became difficult to understand. The conclusion of what he observed is that she no longer wanted him in her department. With the help of FMF, the link person, she wanted to get rid of him. But how was she going to do that? YPY began to frustrate Mr Fox as much as she could. The level of criticism/condemnation increased. It looked like she was in competition with her and she would shoot down any suggestion or contribution that he made in any meeting. Mr Fox stopped contributing in meetings. When he had 100 per cent pass rate in the class of 2009, she remarked this was because he had a top set. In the years that followed, he had residuals, but there was no encouragement or acknowledgement or even mention of those results. Meanwhile, for the following two years or so, he was allocated bottom sets. A veiled description of these bottom sets was that they were a mixed-ability groups (in a class of twenty-one, fifteen or more were SEN or very weak/struggling). Lessons were graded as 'satisfactory', 'satisfactory with some good elements', or, worse still, 'satisfactory with unsatisfactory elements'. Towards the end of his induction period, he could see that she was exasperated. Her combination with FMF had become lethal. On two occasions, the two conducted a joint observation, but FMF would not produce feedback. On another occasion, he challenged the feedback, and YPY told me to go and see FMF, who was a witness in that lesson. The HoD made confessions which he could not understand. She told me that she was not 'confident' to observe me alone; she needed someone in my lessons, so she teamed up with FMF. Fortunately, on no occasion had I argued with the HoD. He said he became even more confused when he realised that the HoD was spearheading my downfall.

Strategy 10 Ms YP and advisors employed an intimidating tactic. JPJ and Ms YPY called him into the latter's office for an interview. Mr Fox felt that this is one of the experiences which was unnerving, if not intimidating, to be interviewed by these two people because he respect them so much. He wondered, however, why the two of them raised the issue of his salary. They left him wondering why they involved themselves in salary issues which he assumed to be private and confidential.

Strategy 11 On another occasion, YPY brought a certain gentleman who had been promoted recently. After introducing him to the class, the gentleman turned to him and asked, 'Are you the gentleman from Zimbabwe?' Mr Fox observed that he does not question the authority of this gentleman in this school. His place of origin was his private life.

Strategy 12 After completing MA, the department was invited for a cup of tea to 'celebrate [my] achievement.' Ms YPY made a mockery of that event when she remarked, 'At least this brings something positive after all that has happened.'

Jonathan Tucker nodded in agreement.

This induction bears the whole marks of institutionalised racism. Evidence presented in this chapter shows that head teachers break the law and get away with it. More importantly, it shows how BME teachers are abused, bullied, and stripped of their rights in a fashion akin to the dark ages of slavery. The evidence shows that the induction process was flawed. In the first instance, it was illegal. They were in breach of the statutory guidance, which clearly says when an OTT has been assessed by the TDA against both the QTS and core standards, the host school has no power to overturn the latter's decision. All the eight assessors did not indicate what they were looking for in their assessments. There was no supervision but assessments only. This is wrong. It is harassment at its worst. The choice of focus for the observations should be informed by (i) the requirements of the core standards and (ii) the NQT's personal objectives for career development' (paragraph 2.70). This was not done. Again, paragraph 2.70 as quoted above requires that 'observations should be supportive and developmental'. None of the eight people who came to assess Mr Fox ever indicated what aspect of classroom management they were focusing on. They were obsessed by the desire to fail him and failed to implement the statutory guide on induction for NQTs.

Mr Fox said he raised concerns about the conduct of the induction process to the borough council, but no action was taken. The council decided to support the head teacher and turn a blind eye to the malpractice which was going on. He raised concerns that the whole induction exercise revolved around a single target C4. Mr Fox informed Mr JMJ that he was actually surprised that the Council had been invited, because he was not aware of any concerns. He was also surprised that he was not aware of the purpose of his visit. He also informed JMJ in the same meeting that he had told Mrs KSK that he was being unjustly treated, racially abused, harassed, and bullied by the head of year, but nothing was done about it. Finally, Mr Fox queried Mrs KSK over the way she was conducting induction on many occasions, and her answer was 'Don't worry. We will get there.'

The good thing that came out of the visit with the Borough Council Representatives was that they discovered the induction was not planned for and therefore served no purpose. More importantly, they were embarrassed to discover the opposite of what they had been told. As a consequence, the school was advised to pass the teacher. For the record, Mrs. Crow came to observe Mr Fox for the first time. This is interesting. When a crisis like the one described in this chapter occurs, the head of school is the one who should intervene, supporting the teacher and devising support strategies. Mrs KSK also came to observe him. She did not grade the lesson but simply said, 'You have done well.' Mr Fox passed the induction after a gruelling struggle. Mrs. Crow should be investigated for breaking the law of induction with impunity, with a premeditated view of trying to destroy someone's life.

CHAPTER 5

CAPABILITY PROCEDURE

Mr Fox informed the author that the head teacher would not rest. He informed me that the head teacher was so vindictive that she would not rest until he had lost his only source of livelihood, teaching. To that end, Mrs. Crow had come up with a strategy of making sure that Mr Fox was stripped of his teaching certificate instituting capability procedure. If she could prove that Mr Fox was a failing teacher, incapable of teaching and monitoring the learning of learners, the government would revoke Mr Fox's teaching certificate. Very competent BME teachers are having their teaching careers ruined by head teachers who do not accept a challenge, especially when it comes from BME teachers. Mrs. Crow engaged **other teachers to do the dirty job of making surveilling** Mr Fox and reporting directly to her office. So head teachers deliberately antagonise teachers under their charge, as they use them to fight their wars with perceived enemies in schools. One might argue that some teachers are gullible, as they are used as hit squads, but most accept that dirty job to hide their own weaknesses. Another possible view is that these teachers were naturally racist. The reader is reminded that, for a period of five years at Cardinal Newman School, the complainant had never had a problem with anyone. He took over a tutor group from Mr EB, who was going to South Africa in 2007. He worked very well with students, parents, and members of staff. The events recorded in this chapter started five years after joining the school and only after he had challenged the head teacher over breach of contract and racial discrimination. The head teacher knew that she could not just dismiss the teacher, for it would be an unfair dismissal. She started building a case against the teacher. She forced the complainant to do an induction (see the chapter on induction above). This was unlawful, but it had to be done so that she would manipulate the induction process and fail the teacher. Alongside the induction, she had to build a record of a struggling teacher so that decisions to discharge the teacher would be easy. An induction would enable her to create evidence of a teacher who was failing an induction so that she would meet the requirement of 6.1 of the 'Statutory Guide on the Induction of Newly-Qualified Teachers in England', section 6.2 'School Teachers' Salary Policy' (2005) (paragraph 4.1, the last part of that section) and 6.3 'School Teachers' Pay and Conditions Document' (2009) (paragraph 18.1.6), which authorises the school to discharge the teacher or withhold some points on grounds of underperformance or incompetence. Mrs. Crow instituted surveillances, bullying, harassment, and dragging in parents to raise issues against the complainant to maximise pressure on the teacher so that the teacher would resign on his own. When the complainant realised that something was wrong in his operations, he raised the issue with the authority. The complainant made a formal complaint to the head teacher over differential treatment he experienced, since he indicated that he was taking the school to the employment tribunal over breach of contract. It is unusual to centralise everything to do with his operation in the head teacher's office, when there is a head of department and head of year. For the first time in seven years, Mr Fox began to experience surveillance on his practice, bullying, harassment, and complaints from parents (most of whom were his workmates).

Indefinite observation: Mrs. Crow co-opted a Mr. Jonathan Tucker (an SLT) to sit in my lessons for a very long time. On 31 January 2011, the complainant received an email from the head teacher informing the complainant that Mr JT was going to sit in my lessons for an indefinite period under the guise of intervention for borderline students (see the email below).

SLT Intervention for C/D Borderline Students (Mr Fox). This letter to Mr Fox has been transcribed

>Dear Mr Fox,
>
>After half term, Mr JT from SLT team will be in your lesson with Year 11 every Monday, Week 1 & Week 2, and Period 1: The role of the SLT member is to:
>
>* To assist the class teacher in teaching the group- similar to a TA role for at least 1 hour.
>* To look at the data provided for the group by Jane Crow and decide (discreetly) which students you are best focusing your attention on
>* Joint responsibility for Assertive Discipline/Behaviour in class
>* Prevent students being sent to Remove if possible by being proactive
>* Make it very obvious that you are helping not observing. There will be no discussion of the teaching outside of the classroom
>* Assist in getting students to hand in work/meet deadlines/attend revision classes/detentions

> * Thank you for your cooperation. Once Year 11 have left I will ask you for brief feedback on how effective you feel this support has been.
>
> Mrs Jane Crow (Head teacher).

The purpose of this strategy was bizarre to say the least. It was difficult to accept that a full-time teacher would find the time to sit in the other teacher's lessons when he was supposed to have his own teaching load. This was tantamount to indefinite lesson observations by Mr Jonathan Tucker. This strategy of gathering information about the complainant created uneasiness among students, who felt that this was an intrusion in their learning. When the classes complained, the programme was discontinued halfway through the term. Earlier, when Mr Fox talked to this gentleman, Mr Tucker about his plight, he had expressed surprise and disbelief. Mr. Fox said that he was surprised to see Mr. Tucker's new role of destroying someone's life.

Another capability procedure was raised over assessment: On 29/05/2011, a gentleman by the name Mr MC came to my classroom and then instructed the head of department to convene a meeting in which the complainant was invited. The purpose of that meeting was to discuss allegations that the complainant does not understand assessment procedures. This allegation came when he had been in the system for five years. The idea was to create records which were documented, because up to this time in point, they had no bad record which they could use against Mr Fox.

Capability procedure over mentoring: Another member of staff (Ms MCL) claimed that Mr Fox did not know how to mentor students, so she insisted that he should observe another member of staff carrying out a mentoring session. This was meant to frustrate the complainant.

Teaching assistants were swopped after the incidents above. A new TA came to support a student in one of his lessons. As soon as she walked in, she started transcribing my lesson instead of supporting the student in question. Mr Fox became concerned that the student was being short-changed, so he informed the SEN coordinator. When he raised concern, MCL changed the complaint. Both the TA and MCL alleged that the TA was compiling information which she was going to use later outside the lesson to support the student concerned. This was obviously not true. Students are supported in the course of the lesson and not later. The TA was compiling notes to be given to MCL for future reference. This was clear victimisation. All this was happening after the employment tribunal to create a record of incompetence, malpractice, and underperformance, the records of which were not available in the five years I had been in this school. This is clear victimisation.

The complainant was charged for responding to the e-mail of the school solicitor: On 22/02/12, he applied for leave of absence to attend an interview and this was granted. During lunch break, the complainant attended to his emails. He replied to the school solicitor's email. The solicitor forwarded the email to the head teacher, who invited him to a meeting, where he was charged and lost income for attending to that email. A record was created, which would be referred to in future. It was unusual for the head teacher to take an audit of how an officer spent the leave of absence here she had applied for. This was clear victimisation. Leave-of-absence policy (2009) allows for 'sufficient leave to attend a job interview'.

Teaching assistants were used for surveillance on the complainant: The head teacher called for a meeting on 17/05/12 to discuss 'concerns raised by TAs who support SEN students in Mr. Fox's classes.' Introducing the agenda of the meeting the head teacher allayed Mr Fox's fears that the meeting had nothing to do with the case under investigation where he took the school to the employment tribunal for discrimination and breach of contract (for details, see the minutes of the meeting). This meeting is significant, as it shows that the head teacher was using TAs to record and or transcribe activities in my lessons and report to the head teacher, which amounts to harassment of the complainant. These minutes are not edited. They are meant to show that this so-called meeting was another way of creating a record about the failures of the complainant.

Mr Fox informed the author that the head teacher was desperate to create records of a struggling teacher because they did not have anything to suggest that he was underperforming. A meeting was therefore convened on 12 May 2012, chaired by the head teacher. Invited to that meeting to be witnesses were other members of staff. Among them was Mr RO (who was representing BME). Ms MC was a member of SLT. The head teacher informed the meeting that it did not have a formal status or disciplinary side to it. She informed members present that there were a few concerns that she wanted to address. These issues were about mentoring and secondly complaints she had received from TAs in Mr Fox's lessons.

Mentoring: Ms MC struggled to introduce the topic because she was aware that this was made up. She informed the meeting that concerns had been raised on both sides of the mentoring process; a number of parents had contacted MCL who were not happy with mentoring meetings and PCD meetings; also, members of staff and other parents had made contact regarding issues with grades on assessments for PCD.

After the first Parents' Consultation Day (PCD) in November, three parents phoned to say that their PCD appointment was very unproductive. They felt you did not know their children, had not developed much of a relationship with their child and when going through assessments, parents were not confident in your interpretation of data. As it was early days parents agreed to give it a bit more time and wait and see. Following March PCD it was felt there was no real improvement in relationships. During the meeting with B's mum and grandmother you said he had a bad report, but in fact you were looking at another student's report. S' report had November and March meetings and parents felt they were just not working and S was getting nothing out of the mentoring process. Also GHN replied to a pink slip and spoke to the parents who explained that a good relationship with their daughter was not possible and she did not feel supported. She felt like you were 'telling her off'. A decision was made to transfer these mentees to someone else.

Regarding the Mentoring Booklets, notes were not made of any meetings in the first term before November PCD. There is evidence of meetings this term. DDY did a review of mentoring and raised concerns that students felt that a relationship was not possible. Mentoring booklets had evidence of this term's meetings, but not last term.

There are also concerns about the information that you are putting on your Music Assessments. Last November you (and other members of staff) gave assessment scores for AM, who had not been in school. For March PCD AOY and PHY were standing in for HFY and when they were conducting meetings with HFY's mentees there were four students with targets of A, B or C, but in their assessments were graded an E or F, but received positive comments. Mentors queried that with a target of A-C, but scoring E or F why did they receive the term 'working hard'. Not really confident that we have cleared up this disparity. On pink slips filled in by yourself, a couple of questions you asked other people to explain to parents were actually things that you, as a mentor, should be explaining to parents.

In conclusion, we are not sure whether you understand the assessment process and completing of reports. Also we have moved four students to other mentors at parents' request. There have been issues with a parent not feeling happy with feedback and explanations. Concerns have also been raised regarding relationships with students.

Mr Fox informed the meeting that, as it regards the process of mentoring, parents have their own interpretation of relationships between myself and students. Mr Fox had designed a questionnaire to establish the level the student is working at, and if they have problems, he had helped quite a number of them. It is not true to say that he mistook students. He had a booking sheet with their names, and he compared that with their report and set targets. There was no issue of mistaking students' names. In addition, he had photographs of students on sheets so he did not confuse them. With as large a group as the one he had, the issue of developing relationships cannot be denied, but at the same time, the parent might feelheI could have done more.

Mrs. Crow enquired if he had meetings with mentees during the first term. The following is a transcription of the meeting minutes, in which Mr Fox answered this question:

Mr Fox: Yes, he wrote something on paper that he could use later. Would build in subject areas and other issues. Next stage was to set targets. While mentoring them on computer and document would ask students questions/concerns/action. Would address items that needed to be addressed. Once or twice may have forgotten to transfer information to booklet, but have all this information. Was meeting them constantly and have records.

Ms MC: Now that you have described the way that the meetings take place he can understand why students did not feel that relationship. Mentoring meetings should be a two-way conversation. Students find it difficult to write things down, and if you are typing it up on a computer you are not talking face to face and you are not building a relationship. Need eye to eye contact. It is important when meeting parents that by asking them to 'fill in a form' you are losing the opportunity to make contact with parents. First impressions are very important.

Mr Fox: About assessment we have new specification for GCSE RE. The questions are in five sections; A = 1; B = 2; C = 3; D = 6; these total twelve and section E = 12. When the department gave first assessment at the beginning of the year the department made the mistake of giving knowledge questions only, to reduce the amount of marking. Mr Fox raised concerns at the time because it was difficult to alter a mark which the student had got. As a result, students got very high marks, with some getting as much as 48/50. That was the grade that was entered on the first assessment. This mark created the wrong impression. The students had not developed enough knowledge and skills to answer the Section E questions which carry half the mark of the whole question marked out of 24.

Mrs. Crow: Did all Music assessment grades have the same problem as you did grading far too high?

Mr Fox: Everybody in Music did this. It has been discussed in the department and has been sorted out. Generally grades have gone down. Grade converters used have made scores even lower. These have been revised again. He mentioned this to parents and students were clear on this. Things have improved greatly since then. Still to complete marking of IS for recent assessments. Have encouraged students to do IS and focus on E question.

Ms MC: Target grades are set at KS2 levels not by internal assessments. The assessment sheet had the following columns: Target at KS2 = A-C;

recent assessment = E or F; Predicted GCSE = predicted up or near to target grade. Your assessment prediction was still E or F.

Mr Fox: As long as the assessment score was close to the target grade as was the case in the October assessment, there was no problem. This issue was not raised in the October assessment because the impression given by the assessment item then was of students who were hitting their targets in the very first term and first assessment of their GCSE. In February the whole group in RE were having a realistic assessment which is used at the end of GCSE. In my professional judgement, giving students an estimated which was close to the target grade would have given the wrong impression that the student is on target when they still have the 12 mark question which even the current year 11 are struggling with. If the requirement is to give an estimated grade close to the target, irrespective of current performance then it is my mistake.

Mrs. Crow: The last column is for a grade that represents, in your professional judgement, if the pupil continues to work at this rate, this is where they will be at GCSE. This helps us to put in interventions. We need to sit down together and see that you understand assessments, particularly that last column. This was coming out in pink slips for teachers.

Mr Fox: Parents were questioning why students were REDs in two consecutive assessments. I tried to explain to them but they insisted that they wanted an explanation from the departments. I therefore referred these to the relevant departments. That is why he raised red slips which required individual teachers to respond or talk to the parent who had raised concerns.

Ms MC: Mentors should explain RAG rating to parents.

Mr Fox: He tried to explain meaning of RAG rating but parents insisted on getting an explanation from the subject teachers concerned in cases where their children had a red.

Ms MC: Need to decide what we need to do to help you improve. Suggestion point – did not understand how score was arrived at.

Mrs. Crow: Do you think it would be helpful to observe a mentoring sessions of a colleague who is getting good reports back from parents? Seeing how they conduct a meeting may help you to change the way you do things. Also could sit down with LMA or MC to go through reports that you are sending through at the moment. MC will pick this up with LM.

Mr Fox informed the author that, out of desperation, the head teacher used teaching assistants to transcribe his lessons so that they would report to the head teacher. Without denigrating these adults, these TAs are not trained teachers, so they cannot see the justification of some strategies the professional teacher may put in place. Most of these are adults in class who have been employed to support and assist on behaviour matters.

Ms MC: Introduced this part by giving the background to Pink Slips. The purpose and justification for Pink Slips is that she cannot be all over the classes where there are SEN learners. TAs use Pink Slips to record and report on what transpires in classes where there SEN learners. So the SEN Department uses Pink Slip system to monitor how SEN students are doing so that if parents have called or if phone calls are made to parents the department has the information to give to parents. These are checked at the end of each week so that I know what is going on.

Mrs. Crow: Last week it was reported that some students in your lessons were struggling. The first pink slip related to a Year 10 Period 6 & 7 lesson. There were some serious issues that were not challenged.

Mr Fox: This group is wrongly constituted. I have raised concerns with YPI and LMA. The TA and I have agreed on several occasions that this group should be reconstituted. There is a small clique of students who have behavioural issues [names supplied]. Then another group of 6 – 8 students who are on the ADHD spectrum who need 1-1 support. Mr Fox informed the meeting that the form of disruption caused by this small group is that they report each other even when nothing has been done just to get each other in trouble. That way they drag the teacher into a debate where one says so and so said this to me and the other person denying it. The other time I received a letter from a parent about one student who claimed a racist remark had been made on him. It turned out that it was not true. To handle this kind of disruption, I have advised them that I need to hear for myself what the other student says before I can act. On the day in question, the boy who claimed that abuse was actually showing off his muscles and body built saying the other person was saying that because of what he saw on him. I have sent these other two to remove several times. I recommended that these students be separated as a long term solution.

Mrs. Crow: There are things happening in this class that should have been addressed with AD. You have got to operate the same system as everybody else. This alerts us to what is going on with these students.

Mrs. Crow: We need to investigate this and get statements from students otherwise it appears to be condoned by you.

Ms MC: TA felt quite exposed and uncomfortable when these issues were not being addressed.

Mrs. Crow: Teacher and TA should share AD in the classroom. You need to explain to students that bad language should not be happening in lessons at all and that it stops. Will talk to Mr LM to alter some of the groups.

Mr Fox: Mr LM has agreed to move JR and WH at the end of half term.

Mrs. Crow: The other pink slip refers to a Year 7 group with HF in. Students need to follow whole school system regarding going to the toilet. They need to be told to go to the toilet before they come to lesson. Lessons also need to be pitched at the students' level.

Ms MC: Does not encourage TAs to comment on teachers.

Mr Fox: It is a question of opinion. Regarding differentiation – trying to reach students through 5 senses. In Music we introduced videos as it helps to explain certain concepts. If the TA does not appreciate the approaches and methods that are used then we have a problem with that TA. I have also intervened on several occasions between FH (student) and the TA concerned when there appeared to be a problem with FH (student) fidgeting around on not being on task.

Mr. Fox: It is not down to TAs to question the structure of the lesson but you need to be alert to the fact that students in this group are struggling and look at the level you are pitching the lesson at. Need to make sure that you are following school systems. At the moment we are just talking about what concerns we have and what support Mr Fox needs to put them right.

What did the head teacher and her team want to achieve?

Ms MC to organise for Mr Fox to observe another mentor.

Mr Fox to ensure Mentor booklets are being filled in.

Ms MC to talk to Mr Fox with Mr LM regarding assessments and ensure Mr Fox understands the Assessment grading system.

Make sure Mr Fox speaks to Year 10 class regarding basic rules of acceptable behaviour in class and uses AD to enforce and prevent unacceptable behaviour and language.

Mr LM to re-constitute Year 10 group.

Year 7 students are not allowed to visit the toilet during lesson.

Mrs. Crow and Ms. MC – after half term observe these two particular lessons to see if things have improved.

Signatures:

Mrs. Crow..
Ms MC ....
Mr Fox ....
Mr RO ....

After going through the minutes above, Mr Fox paused and said this is how evil racism is. In the first instance, these people who were invited were supposed to be witnesses. RO was a union representative. MC was coming to support the head teacher. Allegation after allegation was made. It is significant to note that the head teacher had assumed or taken over the roles of the head of department, deputy head (who was the link to the department), and assistant head (responsible for staff development). The purpose of this meeting was to create a record of the problems which purportedly the complainant was experiencing.

On another incident, some TAs distanced themselves from the SEN coordinator when they realised that they were being used for the wrong reasons. On Tuesday, 19 June 2012, another meeting was convened between the acting HoD, a TA (NB) and Mr Fox. This TA distanced herself from the activities of victimising the complainant using the information she had supplied, arguing that 'it was misconstrued'. They did not realise that the information they were supplying was going to be used to victimise an innocent person.

Mrs. Crow hatched yet another strategy of destroying Mr Fox. She attempted to create capability charge on the complainant by involving parents. One of the SEN coordinators argued that parents had raised concerns about how their children were mentored in the previous Parents' Consultation Day in the previous year, and these concerns were not brought to the attention of the teacher concerned. Some of the parents who were said to have complained were members of the TA's team, which meant the head was deliberately turning other members of staff against the complainant. In his view, using TAs to gather information about a teacher's performance is unprofessional and illegal. The complainant informed the union representative, who challenged administration about the other members of staff, who gathered information about another member of staff.

Another approach employed by Mrs. Crow was to use capability procedure by condemning the lessons of the complainant. A series of impromptu lesson observations were made. On 14/06/12, at 2.30 p.m., two senior members of staff visited Mr Fox lesson during learning walk. He expected this visit because it had been announced. They collected a few exercise books and went away. After a couple of minutes after their departure, the head teacher, Mrs. Crow and Mr. Jonathan Tucker (JT), the assistant head, walked in and made a formal lesson observation. They were in my lesson for fifteen minutes, and they came towards the end of the lesson. The lesson was judged inadequate. This episode on its own carried the marks of clear victimisation. He challenged the assistant head and informed the local union representative on the grounds that (i) this was supposed to be a learning walk, which was turned into a lesson observation, (ii) it was impromptu, (iii) they came towards the end of the lesson and spent less than twenty minutes, (iv) Jane did not give me feedback, (v) the complainant challenged Mr JT on 18/06/12. This was clear victimisation. Mr JT had been used before, on 12/11/2009, when he was invited to support the head teacher, and in that meeting, he had made wild assertions that the claimant could not be placed at M6, as that would be a double-award. This same gentleman teamed up with the head of department on 20/07/11. Mr JT interviewed the complainant about his salary issues and declared that Mrs. Crow could not be wrong. Mr Fox concluded, 'The head teacher was using SLT to victimise me.'

Finally, Mrs. Crow took it upon herself to set targets for performance management for the victim, which is illegal. The head teacher and Ms MC sent a joint statement, dated 28/06/12, informing Mr Fox that they had come up with one of my performance management target which is mentoring, claiming that SLT and parents had raised concerns about the quality of my mentoring. It is unusual for the head teacher to set performance management targets. This was a clear sign of bullying and harassment. The head teacher was becoming confrontational, as she tried to build a case against the complainant in retrospect.

Summarising how he felt as he saw the source of his livelihood slip aware, Mr Fox said he felt like the world had collapsed on him. He had no one to turn to, not even resources to hire lawyers to represent him.

CHAPTER 6

POST-DISMISSAL VICTIMISATION, HARASSMENT, AND BULLYING

Head teachers in England have created a register of offenders which runs parallel with the one run by Home Office for purposes of state security. The head teachers' register is called 'Register of Dismissed Teachers'. When a teacher's name has been posted on this register, he or she will not teach in the United Kingdom again. A head teacher who decides to employ a teacher will check the status of that teacher on the register. Any teacher whose name appears on that register is unemployable. Some enthusiastic head teachers will check your name on the register as you walk into the school if you happen to be a black. Mr Fox told me that he encountered a range of unpleasant treatment from one school to another. The legality of that register is questionable. Whether education secretaries are aware of such a register is another matter, but unions know that such a register exists. No head teacher goes back to that register to delist the teacher because, as Mr Fox's union representative said, it is a lifetime ban once you have been posted on that register. The reader is therefore reminded of Mr Fox's circumstances to see if Mr Fox deserved to be on such a register.

Mr Fox joined Cardinal Newman Secondary School as a supply teacher in January 2007. The head teacher, Mrs. Crow, informed Mr Fox and the employment tribunal,

'When we appointed him he was working for a Supply Agency. The school had to pay £3,525 as recruitment fee for the Claimant becoming a permanent member of staff.' The school therefore employed Mr Fox as an Overseas Trained Teacher with qualifications which are equivalent to UK qualifications according to the UK NARIC certificate he showed me. Mr Fox signed and returned an acceptance of the post. Mrs. Crow the head teacher informed Mr Fox that the issue of salary increase would be discussed after he had completed Qualified Teacher Status (QTS). For the meantime, he would continue of an Unqualified Scale 10 which was the highest pay point for unqualified. Mrs. Crow and Mr Fox discussed how the latter's salary would progress according to the Salary Policy (2005) which he was holding in his hand soon after signing the contract on 5 June 2007. The head teacher showed Mr Fox the relevant sections which outline how his salary was going to progress. A deal was sealed. This policy is at the centre of controversy which led to Mr Fox's dismissal.

After completing QTS on 2 July 2008 Mr. Fox hoped his salary was going to be adjusted in September 2008 according to the 'School Teachers' Salary Policy' (2005), paragraphs 3 (i) 'Starting Salary'; paragraph 3 (ii) 'On Experience'; and paragraph 4 (i) 'On Experience'. I made an appointment to see the head teacher, Mrs. Crow. Mr. Fox joined this school from other schools that had placed me at point 10 of the unqualified (£23,331). After completing QTS, my salary was supposed to rise to M6 (£30,148). When he raised the issue of a discrepancy in my salary, Mrs. Crow made shocking and regrettable statements. Among these documented statements include the following: 'You are not EEA, so you cannot be paid like your counterparts. The school has no money.

After all, we cannot consider your overseas qualifications and experience because they are not recognised here.'

Mr Fox says he challenged her and reminded her that his qualifications were rated as equivalent to UK qualifications by a government department that evaluates and rates overseas qualifications, NARIC, and that they were the same as the rest of the OTTs who had been employed in this school since 2005, eleven of whom came from Colourbar, his country of origin. Mr Fox was therefore dismissed for challenging racist attitudes expressed by the head teacher, Mrs. Crow, and the governor, Mr. Morgan. As events played out, Mr Fox realised that his former employer, Mrs. Crow, unlawfully shared with or distributed information about his dismissal to third party (heads of institutions) with the view to making sure that the complainant is unemployable in the United Kingdom again. Mr Fox argued that Mrs. Crow made an offer with the condition that if the complainant accepted that offer, he would receive a clean reference. Mr Fox believed that because we failed to agree on the unreasonable offer, she knowingly provided a bad reference in order to scare would-be employers away from employing the complainant. Mr Fox further observed that Mrs. Crow had, in agreement with other head teachers, agreed to place the complainant on a register of sacked teachers, an 'offenders registers', so that he would not be employed in the UK the rest of his life. As events show below, I have been offered teaching posts in a number of schools, only to be told later, 'We no longer need you' as soon as they verified my identity. The reader is once again reminded that the records in this chapter have nothing to do with individual head teachers. The evil and racist attitude should be exposed.

In including this chapter in this book, Mr Fox believes that head teachers are agencies of racial integration. They have among their curriculum Citizenship and PSHE, both of which are intended to develop and inculcate values which should enable learners to live in harmony in a multicultural, multiracial, and multiethnic society, and yet head teachers are the culprits of racism. The records below tell a full story about the extent to which they measure to that challenge.

The issue of racism in the education sector is a public phenomenon following the evidence presented to Parliament in a report by teachers' unions. In 2017, Runnymede, NASUWT, and Act for Racial Justice published the report, 'Visible Minorities, Invisible Teachers: BME Teachers in the Education System in England', which presented the NASUWT big-question survey findings, alongside other research, evidencing poor experiences across the school system for BME teachers, with discrimination and unequal treatment starting early in teachers' careers, with lower pay on average than peers, amid a pervasive culture of racism.

The register of sacked teachers in the UK is another sign of the ugly face of institutionalised racism in the United Kingdom. Legal or illegal, some head teachers are monsters who still uphold that a teacher from the BME background is inferior, second class, and without rights. The report presented to Parliament by unions and activists is enough evidence that Mr Fox's case is not an isolated incident. As an aside, the Windrush story exposed Home Office in that, it was discovered that, for years, people from the Caribbean were being deported unlawfully. Similarly, many BME teachers are relegated to relying on council benefits when they should working for themselves and contributing to the economy. This is a sad story.

Mr Fox recorded his unpleasant experiences of trying to get a job after the dismissal. Five years went by where he could not be employed even though his DBS (or CRB) was clean. The evidence below is proof that a single head teacher can make an unreasonable decision which ruins lives of a BME teacher,, and other head teachers will agree unanimously to put that innocent teacher on an 'never-employ-him-or-her register'. This register is secretly kept by the schools so that even if the teacher is invited for interviews and performs very well in both the interview and lessons observed, the feedback one receives is 'He has done very well, but we do not want him here.' Or they may say, 'The post has been withdrawn.'

In some schools, I was ordered to leave and escorted out of their premises as soon as they discovered it was me. The events recorded below are indisputable.

Mr Fox said the first sign of institutionalised racism came from one of the school he had served in 2006. Mr Fox said he was on a closed contract covering maternity leave. When he joined Cardinal Newman School, he used a good reference from the head teacher of that school. It is therefore important to note that before this controversy between Mrs. Crow and him over the issue of salary, MRUS had always provided a clean reference for the him. He was shocked to learn from a teaching agency on 09/02/13 that the head teacher of MRUS had refused to give a reference to the agency, arguing that they no longer had his records. The head teacher of MRUS continued to refuse to provide a reference to teacher agencies arguing that he no longer remembered Mr Fox. Some of the reasons he gave were that it is a long time ago since he left the school. This is obviously an excuse. This was influence from Cardinal Newman School in support of each other. I believe that this head teacher was unreasonable. Mr Fox sent the head teacher his contract with Mrs. Crow and her emails, in which she rejected his qualifications as reasons for not honouring their contract. This head teacher did not respond. Mr Fox concluded from this episode that head teachers support their own just for the sake of it, something they would not do in the event that the victim was a white EEA.

Mrs. Crow refused to provide a reference to agencies that tried to get me a job. The agencies mentioned below are witnesses to the vindictiveness of Mrs. Crow. She vowed that even when she left Cardinal Newman School, whoever took over would not provide clean references. Indeed, the agencies below would testify. The head teacher instructed everyone who sought for a reference NOT to commit anything in writing. There are a few who have unwittingly disclosed that both head teachers are refusing to give a reference. On 11/02/2013, TT informed Mr Fox that they were not allowed to give you the actual copy of the reference. I can confirm that the reference from Grey School states that you were dismissed and that RUS refused to give you a reference. On 14/010/2013 EdL wrote to Mr Fox that they had received back two references from your referees. Unfortunately, they are limited in content. Mr Fox told me that Mrs. Crow was ruining his life by placing his name on the list of sacked teachers. Mr Fox said he was not aware of a law which criminalises refusing a reference. What is criminal is to post a teacher's name on the sacked or dismissed teachers' register. Mr Fox narrated his ordeal with schools as he tried to get a job. His experiences were very unpleasant as he narrated them.

Mr Fox first went to TMUS as a supply teacher to cover a teacher who had had problems. He was reliably informed by another member of the department that the teacher he was covering was not coming back. He supplied for one week only. The agency phoned on Friday that the school no longer needed me. The school posted an advertisement in the local newspapers 16/10/2011 and 27/10/11 for a Music teacher. He submitted his application in a recorded and monitored delivery. There was no acknowledgement. The post was re-advertised. He applied again but there was no response. This cannot be a coincidence. As this manuscript was being compiled, the school had an advertisement which was running, but Mr Fox said he could no longer be bothered to apply because he tried three times without even an acknowledgement by the school to say they had received the application.

This is institutionalised racism.

Next Mr Fox submitted an application to SUS again in the local community who had posted an advertisement for a post of a Music teacher between 12/04/12 and 03/05/12. He submitted his application in a recorded and monitored delivery. There was no acknowledgement. The post was re-advertised between 11/09/12 and 27/09/12 in the local paper. He applied again using the same method, but there was no response. Mr Fox first surmised that SUS did not want to employ BME teacher. He then realised that this could not been the case, because he knew one BME teacher in that school who had trained overseas. Mr Fox strongly believes that he was the most suitable candidate for that post. He has relevant qualifications up to A level, has relevant experience, and has a record of producing excellent results from his previous school. His conclusion was that this school had information about him from Mrs. Crow. This is the ugly face of institutionalised racism.

Mr Fox's next experience was painful. He attended an interview at SJA in the neighbouring town on 12 July 2013. The interview went on very well. After the interview, the teacher was offered the teaching post. He was also informed of his teaching load and starting date pending receipt of a reference. When SJA contacted his former school, the post was withdrawn. He was informed by phone that the school had withdrawn the post. Again this is the ugly face of institutionalised racism.

Next, an agent by the name KD sent an email on Thursday, 5 September 2013. She assured Mr Fox that RS school in the neighbouring town had arranged an interview for him. He was told who to contact of on arrival in the school. All the groundwork had been laid. In their discussion, she had informed Mr Fox that the position was for a teacher of RE up to A Level. All the work had been set, so there was no planning involved. The school just wanted to observe him in a lesson to see his teaching style and interaction with the children. KD said she had really sold his experience to them on the basis that he had been a head of department and also had long service in the schools he worked in and made a real difference with regards to raising attainment levels for the students and making a difference in each school he worked in. She assured Mr Fox, 'The Music department are really looking forward to seeing you on Monday. As discussed, it will be for a full-day teaching/trial day, and you will be paid for this day. I really wish you the best of luck, Fox, on Monday, and I really hope you are successful. Please do call me if you have any questions before Monday about the position. Have a lovely weekend.'

So again, Mr Fox attended that interview at RSW on 9 September 2013. The interview was scheduled for the whole day. There was a bit of a drama on that day. Mr Fox met the head teacher and two other members of the senior management team (SLT) in the head teacher's office. He was then led to the classroom, where he was supposed to spend the day. As he was teaching his first lesson, someone was waiting to inform him that he was no longer wanted in this school. The interview was abandoned halfway through. This is how institutionalised racism manifests itself.

Out of desperation, Mr Fox was prepared to travel long distances, hoping he would get to regions where his name was new. Another agency arranged a teaching post at STB on 7 October 2013. The deputy head teacher informed him that there were four vacancies in the Music department waiting to be filled in. They were in a very desperate and precarious situation. Mr SK persuaded him to join them. The agency told him they were organising their timetable and it was a matter of days before they contacted them. After teaching for one week, the agency phoned him on a Friday after school to say, 'The school no longer wants you. You should not go back there on Monday.' Mr Fox had to post the keys of the classroom together with textbooks. While he experienced these embarrassing moments in his life, he was saddened to notice classes of GCSE students who were also sacrificed because they were left with no teacher as they were preparing for examinations. This is how toxic racism can be.

Mr Fox was beginning to lose hope on his teaching career, so he was prepared to do any job to protect his family. He therefore attended an interview at SERCO on 16 September 2013. Mr Fox went through a very rigorous and challenging assessment, which a number of people had failed. The interview was organised in such a way that one had to pass several tests before they qualify for the final round of a face-to-face interview. On the day of the interview itself, Mr Fox discovered that his name had been crossed out on the list of interviewees. The lad who was taking details of those people who had passed could not explain why his name had been crossed out. 'The reason why his name was been crossed out is that, on my application form, he had indicated he had been dismissed from his previous job for standing up for my rights. Although he was among the few who passed the interview, he received regret on the following day, 17 September 2013.' What reasons for dismissing Mr Fox could there have been so that even the prison service could not employ him? This is the ugly face of institutionalised racism.

Another vacancy came up at a school in the nearby town. Mr Fox informed me that what happened at this school proved beyond any doubt that SJHS had information about him. Once again, Mr Fox attended an interview for a permanent Music position, as usual. He began with a face-to-face interview with three SLTs in the deputy head's office. 'They expressed satisfaction with my performance,' he noted. He was then escorted to the Music department where he received a warm welcome from the head of department. The lady showed him what was going to be his classroom. That was the classroom he used for his observed lesson. They informed him that they were going to talk to the agency for the final contract details. On his way out, he tried to see the deputy head, but she was no longer as enthusiastic to talk to him. He assumed that she was busy, so he left. One week passed before he received the timetable and resources. In the second week, the agency phoned to say the school had changed their mind. Is this not incredible? This is the ugly face of institutionalised racism. Head teachers of these schools cannot be absolved of wrongdoing, because they should demand adequate detail of what happened to sentence a professional person to a lifetime ban.

What happened at the next school is unbelievable. An agency organised an interview for an Music position at MWSS on Tuesday 18 April 2017. Mr Fox met the head of department, a Mrs JM, who observed his lesson and then organised a timetable for him. Mr Fox said he 'felt the head of department did not look enthusiastic about me joining them'. He also felt that the school was just desperate for a Music teacher. If they had a choice, they would not have taken him for that term. Mr Fox started immediately and worked very well throughout the term. 'The contract was not clear until end of term, when he realised that he had to look for a job.' They interviewed one or two teachers for Music while he was still there. This is the ugly face of institutionalised racism.

The whole mark of institutionalised racism is that people stop to think and ask moral questions. Is it right? Mr Fox's experiences in the next school are a sad story to share with parents, because their children once again are sacrificed in the process of fixing an innocent teacher. Mr Fox informed the author that while he was at MWS, KD, from the agency mentioned above, arranged an interview for a Music teacher on 13 July 2017 at WAS. There was a little drama at this school. Mr Fox was instructed to meet the head teacher's PA. He waited for her, but she was nowhere to be seen, until a head of faculty came to escort him to the Humanities department, where he was handed over to the head of department. The head of department was excited as we went through the structure of the department while he was waiting for students to come from break. He intimated to Mr Fox that the class he was to teach was a bit challenging, so he was to expect anything. Towards the end of the lesson, the head of faculty came and enjoyed the last part of the lesson. He was expecting a face-to-face interview but was told to go when we got to the reception. He was surprised. The head of faculty could not hide his embarrassment too. So the interview was not completed. Institutionalised racism contaminates everyone like cholera. In the end, people develop hatred whose origin and cause are unknown to them.

The next event is interesting. There must have been a reason why this happened. The following Thursday, 20 July 2017, another agency phoned with the exciting news that there was a school that was desperate for a Music teacher who could teach up KS 5. She gave Mr Fox directions to the school while he was busy with end of term preparations. Mr Fox drove from MWSW straight to that school in a nearby town. He only realised that he had been invited to the same school a week before. He phoned the agency with the news that he had been to this school the week before. The agency put him on hold and phoned the school who told them that they did not want me. These schools sacrifice students for their selfish cause.

As we were busy compiling this chapter, Mr Fox showed me an email from a member of the agency, KD, who was pleading with him to go to school because they had not found a teacher for that subject but there are certain teachers they do not want in their schools. This begs the question: Do head teachers stop to think about the impact of their actions on the innocent schoolchildren, or are they so blinded by racism that they would rather not have a particular teacher in their school?

Mr Fox informed the author that on 31 September 17, he received a call from an excited agency, JG, who went as far as to congratulate him for successfully securing him a half-day trial at a nearby school called CVG. JG congratulated Mr Fox and gave him the details of the school. The interview was going to be conducted by the head of department's assistant head teacher (KG). 'They would then like you to deliver a one-hour music lesson to a group of mixed-ability students,' he was told. The details provided in the email show that this school was serious and they definitely wanted a teacher as soon as possible. After the interview in the assistant head teacher's office, teaching was just a formality. The head of department was already preparing topics he was supposed to handle the following Monday. Mr Fox said as he was nearing the end of his lesson delivery that KG dashed out to her office as if to check on something. After the lesson, he was escorted out of the school. A few hours after the interview, JG phoned to say, 'They were impressed with your performance in the interview and in the lesson, but they said they do not want you.' JG asked if there was something wrong because that feedback was unusual. Mr Fox said he did not know what the problem was.

On a lighter note, Mr Fox joked about his experiences with the next school, JFKSH. He had the impression that the head teacher and head of department just wanted to see the person, Mr Fox. They invited him, the agency said, 'to chat'. The agency assured Mr Fox in an email on 19 September 2017 that, as discussed, the school are looking for a Music teacher to work three days a week, starting in September, initially until Christmas but with the potential to continue. 'We can also offer you a place on our guaranteed work scheme in September, which means that if we do not find you work for the other two days, then you will still be paid. The head of department would like to meet with you tomorrow for an informal chat about the role and go over the timetable for September.'

Mr Fox attended the meeting on 20 July 2017 at 11.30 a.m., as arranged. He met two SLT, one of whom could have been the head of department. The chat was too general to be meaningful. After a couple of hours, the agency phoned to say they do not want him. Mr. Fox said he had a feeling that they just wanted to see my face only.

Mr Fox informed the author that he could go on and on giving many more examples of how institutionalised racism operates in schools. He, however, felt that he could not ignore his experiences at this next institution. His experiences at the next school were unique. He was offered a two-term contract by this school after attending an interview. He was covering maternity, and one more lady in that department was due for maternity leave. Besides, another member of staff in that department had just left. It was therefore clear to him that in one way or another, the school needed a full-time teacher. 'This was an opportunity for me to be offered full-time employment this time around. The head of department is second to none. We worked very well for that reason; he encouraged me to apply for this post when it comes up.' Towards the end of the first term, the post of full-time Music teacher was advertised. Mr Fox applied for the post. On the day of the interview, he discovered that there were two interviewees. The school appointed an outsider, a young lady. Logically a forward-planning head teacher makes such decisions. The difficulty, however, is that you advertise a post when already there is someone whom you engaged after an interview. You invite the incumbent to attend another interview for the same post he had been interviewed before he was employed earlier. Then, in the second round of interviews, that teacher 'underperforms'. It's a dicey one. 'Be that as it may, I felt betrayed and unwanted.' Mr Fox said he could almost hear the echoing voice of Mrs. Crow when she vowed that he would never teach in England again. Did the head teacher check the sacked teachers register? If the head teacher made this decision based on my circumstances, was he not supporting a racist head teacher? If he appointed the younger lady, was he not guilty of ageism? Mr Fox spoke with a very low and dejected voice when he said, 'Whichever way one looks at it, these organisations were discriminatory in their recruitment method. My conclusions from these experiences were that the organisations were following their instinct, to support their counterpart, the white head teacher, against a black person who had no right to challenge the decisions of the head teacher.'

The behaviour outlined in Mr Fox's experiences with the head teachers makes it difficult to absolve them from a possible crime of racism. Signing to and using information from an organisation or website which they knew was created specifically to destroy lives make them accomplices. The other issue readers might want to explore is the legality of that register. Was it created for security? Whose security? Is the state aware of the existence of such a register? If the state is not aware of the existence of such a register, then it is a crime to ban someone from practising when DBS is clean. Last but not least, why is there no appetite on the part of the state to deal with this problem? It is disheartening to note that the issue of racism in the education sector is a public phenomenon following the evidence presented to Parliament in a report by teachers' unions. In 2017, Runnymede, NASUWT, and Act for Racial Justice published the report, 'Visible Minorities, Invisible Teachers: BME Teachers in the Education System in England', which presented the NASUWT big-question survey findings, alongside other research, evidencing poor experiences across the school system for BME teachers, with discrimination and unequal treatment starting early in teachers' careers, with lower pay on average than peers, amid a pervasive culture of racism. Mr Fox said, 'It is frustrating to realise that BME teachers are not guaranteed for secure in their jobs if Parliament cannot investigate such an important issue, which was tabled in Parliament. Racism and racially motivated crime is a pandemic in the United Kingdom which needs to be investigated. What makes this issue complex is that, the head teachers, council departments, the legal institutions and Parliament seem to protect offenders or perpetrators of racism at the expense of the victim.' This is the mark of institutionalises racism in the United Kingdom.

CHAPTER 7

THE EMPLOYMENT TRIBUNAL SERVED THE INTERESTS OF THE WHITES: THIS CASE REVEALS

This chapter is dedicated to members of the British Community who may be concerned about racism and its negative impact on the innocent peace loving citizens of all races. Racism is a crime in the United Kingdom. What is racism? The Race Relations Act 1965 was the first legislation in the United Kingdom to address racial discrimination. **This act outlawed discrimination on the grounds of colour of skin, race, or ethnic or national origins.** Research has been conducted by Unions in the education sector to establish the prevalence, extent or severity of racism in the education system. In 2017, Runnymede, NASUWT, and Act for Racial Justice published the report 'Visible Minorities, Invisible Teachers: BME Teachers in the Education System in England', which presented the NASUWT big-question survey findings, alongside other research, evidencing poor experiences across the school system for BME teachers, with discrimination and unequal treatment starting early in teachers' careers, with lower pay on average than peers, amid a pervasive culture of racism. Head teachers flout with impunity their school salary policies and teachers pay and conditions service. An overseas teacher is not paid as well as his or her white counterpart. Overseas-trained teachers are not given the same promotion opportunities as their white counterparts. The case of Mr Fox sadly mirrors the above research which was conducted by Teachers Unions. The sad thing is that perpetrators of crime of racism as defined above, are protected by the justice system and the complainant is literally victimised for challenging racism.

This chapter collates all the evidence of racism expressed openly, insinuated, documented, and acted upon against Black and Ethnic Minority teachers in the United Kingdom. The author will expose evidence which show the hypocrisy of the Employment Tribunal as they dealt with Mr Fox's claims of racism. The purpose of this section of the book is to make the public aware that racism is not confined to football, the health sector, but in the most unlikely of places, the education sector but the ET looks away and punishes Claimants.

Mr Fox presented these documentary Evidence to the Employment Tribunal.

Mr Fox joined Cardinal Newman Catholic School as a supply teacher. The school decided they could not lose him so they paid £3525 recruitment fees to an agency. (doc 1). This is an extract from the head teacher's witness statement to the ET, informing the latter about the true status of the complainant. Having scrutinised Mr Fox's original certificates and the National Recognition Certificate (NARIC), the school was satisfied with Mr Fox's qualifications (doc 4) they offered him a standard contract of employment was signed **(doc 2)**. Mr Fox was given the school salary policy **(See appendix)**. These documents are crucial if anyone wants to understand how head teachers who are racist discriminate BME teachers. When one signs a contract one is informed how they are going to be remunerated. The ET judges will agree if not support the school's solicitors who argue in a wayward, rejecting the provisions of that policy. If the school does not have two salary policies, one for EEA teachers and the other one for BME, they should examine paragraphs **3: Starting Salary of New Appointments, 3.i -3.iv and paragraph 4 Experience.** Mrs Jane Crow was asked by Mr Fox if she has two separate salary policies. She informed the ET judge that she did not. The judge looked away and pretended not to have heard anything discriminatory about that admission. **The judge served the interests of Whites instead of standing up for justice.**

Mr Fox enroled for Qualified Teacher Status (QTS) which he completed QTS in July 2008 (doc 6). The attention of the reader is drawn to two important factors. The Teacher Development Agency (Not the school) together with the Governors scrutinised the content of Mr Fox's degrees, hired an outsider to further determine if Mr Fox was qualified to do this accreditation course (QTS) with exemption from induction. **This information is crucial because the head teacher misleads Governors that Mr Fox received his Initial Teacher Training (ITT) at Cardinal Newman Catholic School (CNCS) which is false.** By the time Mr Fox finished his accreditation course, the school had employed as many as 20 Overseas Trained Teachers some of whom had moved on **(doc 5)**. The head teacher, governors and solicitors later mislead the ET that they did not recognise Mr Fox's teaching qualifications. They would argue that Mr Fox received his ITT in 2008, the year when he completed QTS at CNCS. Mr Fox challenged them to disclose the full list of Overseas Trained Teachers past and present but they refused. The ET ignored all applications for disclosure. **In this case the ET served White interests.**

*According to the school teachers' salary policy (2005), paragraph 3 (i) starting salary, paragraph 3 (ii) on experience, and paragraph 4 (i) on experience (see the highlighted sections of the policy above) Mr Fox was supposed to be awarded a maximum of 6 points in recognition of his long service in education. This did not happen. So he approached the office of the head teacher **(See appendix).** That correspondence constitute the first step in the school grievance procedure. Mrs. Crow was adamant that she was not going to apply the salary policy as quoted above. But what was racist in her response?

The responses which came from the authorities were racist in nature

Most of the responses are recorded above in chapter 1. Of public interest and therefore concern are the four (4) documents which are quoted here. In an email to Mr Fox on 15 June 2011 @ 15:20 Mrs. Crow wrote, 'Thank you for this information. However, we have to write in the experience from the point of view of when you gained QTS in this country as your previous qualifications were not recognised here'**(See appendix)**. This is discrimination based on origin of nationality. One of the governors wrote, Jane said it is your qualifications which are not recognised according to national policy (See appendix). A Linda Scuder, representing governors also wrote to the ET, 'Jane was clear that although we accept your NARIC certificate, we do not recognise your teaching qualifications' **(See appendix).** Finally, the chair of governors Mr Andy Morgan wrote, 'You were not entitled to a higher scale as your previous experience is not in one of the institutions listed in the guidance and policy documents…' **(See appendix).** This evidence of racism should be worrying to the British community. The Employment Tribunal did not want to entertain these documentary evidence. **In this regard, the ET served the interests of Whites.**

Mr Fox tried to argue that he was not the only OTT teacher in school. He wanted to make a comparison of the 20 other OTTs who were employed by the school between 2000 and 2012, 8 of whom were still in school **(doc 5)**. Among these teachers, four (4) of them trained at the same university and same period as Mr Fox. The ET ignored several applications for disclosure **(See appendix).** These correspondences show the hypocrisy of the ET. They did not only ignore Mr Fox's applications but expressed frustration. With this level of support from the ET, the school solicitors defied ET orders of disclosure and openly declared that they would not disclose names of these teachers **(See appendix). By permitting the school to refuse disclosure, when the case was based on that information, the ET served the interests of the Whites.** The ET went a step further to prop up the perpetrators of racism by seting up Pre-hering Reviews which created a new and distorted claim. These pre-hearing Reviews were initiated either by the ET judges or the solicitors. The claim before the ET of race discrimination (paragrapg 5.1b) **(See appendix)** was changed to 'unlawful deductions'. Suffice to say this claim was dismissable. The ET adjudicated on the wrong claim 'unlawful deduction of earnings.' The judge then laid out issues they were going to deal with:

(i) Whether the Tribunal has jurisdiction to consider that complaint having regard to the relevant time limit **(the judge dismissing racism)**

(ii) Whether the Respondent's employment of the Claimant on point M3 in September 2008 was on grounds of race (the judge dismisses race discrimination and the salary policy paragraph 3.i -3.iv and paragraph 4). This is a sad situation.

By creating a new claim through PHRs and rejecting evidence that the head teacher had abandoned their salary policy, the ET was serving the interests of Whites.

It is difficult to absolve the ET of corruptly propping up the school so that Mr Fox's case would be dismissed. To dismiss future reference to the dictates of the salary policy as quoted above, the school resorted to changing the contract (docs 23 and 24). The head teacher made three offer letters (12 June 2007; 21 August 2007; and 10 September 2008). When Mr Fox raised that issue showing these documents to the Judge, he was rebuked. The school also created acceptance letters (25 June

2007; 25 June 2007; 18 September 2007; and 13 September 208) with forged signatures. Mr Fox further showed the ET judge five Statements of Particulars all of which had contradicting information. Again Mr Fox raised concern and proved to the ET judge that two acceptance letters with the same dates show that the signatures were forged. Once again the Judge looked away and proceeded to accept all those documents as if there was nothing wrong. When Mr Fox insisted that he recognised only one contract that he signed with the head teacher and not the rest of these documents, the Judge remarked, 'Why would someone sign so many contracts anyway?' Mr Fox informed the author that, he was saddened to witness the Judge proceeding to dismissing his case. In this instance, the Judge was not concerned about serving justice to this case but to protect the head teacher when he realized the gravity of the matter before him. It is therefore evident that the ET served the interests of Whites when he ignored this set of evidence.

The ET missed several opportunities to deliver a judgement which should have absolved the justice system from this corruption. First, when a contract has been signed, it binds the two parties to the demands and requirements therein. Documents 1, 2, and 3 should have been respected as evidence enough by the Judge that there was something wrong. Instead, the Judge accepted or looked away as the school presented new contracts. Secondly, the Judge was presented with documented racist statements (docs 19; 22.1; 25 and 26) but he looked the other way. Third, the school claimed that they did not recognise Mr Fox's qualifications because they had been obtained overseas. Mr Fox argued that this ruling could not apply to him alone where twenty one (21) Overseas Teachers had been employed by the school. He therefore applied for disclosure. Documents 43 shows unequivocally the school refusing to comply with both the ET and County Court orders. There was need for a comparator. The Judges looked away. Further still, the school changed the contract, forging signatures, some documents being presented in duplicate or triplicate, the Judges looked away. By creating a new claim (unlawful deduction of salary) through PHRs and rejecting evidence that the head teacher had abandoned their salary policy, the ET was serving the interests of Whites. Mr Fox concluded from just these sets of evidence that indeed, the Employment Tribunal is there to serve the interests of the White people and not to protect the weak Black Minority Ethnic groups.

After the ET hearing which dismissed a case they had created during PHRs, Mr Fox was dismissed from work. The trumped up charged were, 1) **'You made false, inaccurate and misleading statements: 2) You mad vexatiuos and malicious and/or frivolous complaints,…'.** This marked the end of Mr Fox's road in the United Kingdom. From here on, his profession was thrown into the bin. He became unemployable. When racism is institutional, it becomes very difficult to eradicate. Black and Minority Ethnic people will forever suffer under the remnants of colonialism. Today Mr Fox is unemployable because his name has been spread on the internet for everyone to see. See the websites below. It is this falsefication of information which prompted the writing of this book providing documentary evidence. This book should shame the analysis below because it is based on false information and has ruined Mr Fox's life. https://www.employmentcasesupdate.co.uk/site.aspx?i=ed26763 or https://www.localgovernmentlawyer.co.uk/employment/312-employment-features/25904-employees-who-lose-tribunal-claims This is a false analysis of Mr Fox's case based on false information and compared to the evidence of racism above shows that the ET is in breach of GDRP. That analysis has been appended in this book.

Reflections of the oppressed: The 'Me Too' movement in America has changed lives of many women in that part of the world and in other democracies across the world. If women who were abused in the entertainment industry kept quiet, the plight of innocent women trying to get a living would have continued. One woman, two women, and more cried out and galvanised into a movement, which has seen the most powerful and untouchable men face justice. In a similar vein, this book is meant to be the mouthpiece of BME teachers who have been abused, discriminated against, and called names in the United Kingdom and across the entire world when they faithfully and professionally conducted themselves to serve the nations. Unions and activists have played their part of presenting this issue to Parliament, but the latter have no appetite to institute Parliamentary investigations and bring to book perpetrators of breaking the statutes of Parliament. The book also should work as an impetus to teachers of all races, colour, creed, gender, faith, and political affiliation in schools across the United Kingdom to challenge foul play where they see it. It is also hoped that people in authority who read this book might see and reflect on their shortfalls and act fast to restore the image of BME teachers in the education system. We also wish that an investigation should be carried out about the legality of the 'offenders register' which is run by head teachers. In progressive society like the United Kingdom, it is common knowledge that offenders who commit very serious crimes like murder are given a sentence which they serve and are given the second chance. Head teachers ban for life any teacher who dares challenge their prejudices. The reader is encouraged to think very carefully about Mr Fox's plight. If you are affected by it, please share this with as many people as you can reach. Mr Fox may not be the only one in this situation. If you know someone who is affected by Mr Fox's experiences, direct them to contact the publishers of this book so that the BME teachers, and indeed all progressive British people, speak with a louder voice to protect BME teachers. Unions on their own cannot win this war on racism, which is supported and nourished by head teachers, bodies of governors, councils, and even the justice system. This is what has prompted the author in consultation with Mr Fox to include the identities of the main players in the Mr Fox's odeal.

https://www.employmentcasesupdate.co.uk/site.aspx?i=ed26763 or

VUPENYU waMWAMBA

https://www.localgovernmentlawyer.co.uk/employment/312-employment-features/25904-employees-who-lose-tribunal-claims

Qualified Teacher Status

This is to certify that:

Morrison Ngwenya

Teacher Reference Number: **0612414**

has attained qualified teacher status (QTS), and meets the requirements for employment in maintained schools and non-maintained special schools in England provided that a statutory induction period (usually three school terms) is completed satisfactorily.

DATE OF QTS: **2 July 2008**

Congratulations and best wishes for your future career.

Doc 6 - Qualified Teacher Status (QTS)

VUPENYU waMWAMBA

Induction

Induction

This is to certify that:

Morrison Ngwenya

Teacher Reference Number: **0612414**

has successfully completed a statutory induction period at a maintained school, non-maintained special school, independent school or sixth-form college. The holder of this certificate is a qualified teacher and has obtained the required qualifications and completed the necessary training for the profession of school teacher in England.

DATE INDUCTION COMPLETED: **22nd July 2009**

Congratulations and best wishes for your future career.

Judy Moorhouse

Chair of the General Teaching Council for England

GTC
General Teaching Council for England

IND0113812

Doc 7 - Induction

The Ugly Face of Institutional Racism

Judy Moorhouse, Chair
Keith Bartley, Chief Executive

Our ref: TQ – EBRhome.0612414

18 July 2008

Mr. M Ngwenya
29 Acacia Road
Bedford
MK42 0HT

Victoria Square House
Victoria Square
Birmingham B2 4AJ
Email: TQhelpdesk@gtce.org.uk
Telephone: (0870) 001 0308
Facsimile: (0121) 345 0100
Website: www.gtce.org.uk

Dear Mr. Ngwenya

On behalf of the General Teaching Council for England (GTC) may I congratulate you on gaining Qualified Teacher Status and welcome you to the teaching profession. I am pleased to enclose your QTS certificate. You will find your Teacher Reference Number on your certificate and this should be referred to by your employer, and when dealing with Teacher Pensions and the GTC.

You must be registered with the GTC if you are a qualified teacher and you are employed to carry out 'specified work' in a maintained school, a non-maintained special school or a pupil referral unit.

'Specified Work' is defined as:
- Planning and preparing lessons and courses for pupils;
- Delivering lessons to pupils;
- Assessing the development, progress and attainment of pupils; and
- Reporting on the development, progress and attainment of pupils.

The requirement to register applies to full-time, part-time and supply teachers. If you are employed as a teacher in other settings, it may be a requirement of your contract of employment that you are registered with the GTC. You should check this with your employer.

You will also find enclosed an application to register form to be completed in full. Please note we will only process registration applications accompanied by a completed direct debit instruction. Once registered, you will be sent written confirmation and a registration card.

All registered teachers are required to make arrangements to pay the annual registration fee. The fee year runs from April to March. The registration fee for 2008/2009 will be £33 payable from 1 April 2008.

If you have any queries about the GTC, please contact us via our website www.gtce.org.uk or on 0870 001 0308.

Yours sincerely

Alan Meyrick
Registrar

Enc

Whenever you contact us, to help us respond quickly and accurately to your enquiry, please provide your full name, date of birth and Teacher Reference Number or National Insurance Number, and quote the reference from our correspondence.

INVESTOR IN PEOPLE

Doc 8 - General Teaching Council

3. **STARTING SALARY OF NEW APPOINTMENTS**

   I. The Governing Body has adopted the local agreement in respect of the assessment of teachers' pay. The starting salary for all new entrants to the teachers' pay spine without previous teaching or relevant industrial, professional or research experience will be at point M1.

   II. Where the new entrant to the profession has experience which may count towards salary, points will be awarded as follows:

   By reference to paragraph 3(I) above, plus points in respect of teaching service and industrial, professional and research experience considered to be of value in the performance of the teacher's duties on the basis of 1 point in respect of each complete period of 2 years.

   New entrants to the profession are required to complete the equivalent of three terms satisfactory induction. Successful completion enables continuous eligibility for employment as a teacher. Failure to complete successfully the induction period, will result in the termination of employment in accordance with the Education (Induction Arrangements for School Teachers) (England) Regulations 1999).

   III. The Governors will continue to seek the assistance of the Authority to verify teachers' qualifications and previous experience for salary purposes.

   IV. Qualified teachers taking up a new appointment, or who re-enter teaching after a break in service, will be paid on a point on the teachers' pay spine no lower than the point on which they were last being paid calculated by reference to the teacher's qualifications and experience. This calculation will be carried out whether the teacher was previously employed on a regular full-time or part-time or occasional supply basis. Where the Governing Body employs a qualified teacher as a classroom teacher who was last employed as a Headteacher or Deputy Headteacher or Assistant Headteacher, appointment will be to the first point of the upper pay spine (plus any additional allowances), U1, provided that the teacher has worked in that capacity for a minimum of three years or was employed in that capacity prior to 1 September 2000. A classroom teacher who was previously employed as an AST will revert to the first point of the upper pay spine (U1).

4. **EXPERIENCE**

   I. The Governing Body will award up to six points for experience. A teacher (including a part-time or occasional supply teacher) would be eligible for an experience point for each school year in which the teacher has taught for part of at least 26 weeks or was due to but was prevented from doing so for reasons of sickness, maternity or some other absence acknowledged by the Governing Body. Experience as a qualified teacher within an Education Action Zone, MOD school or as an AST will be taken into account in determining eligibility for experience points. The Governing Body acknowledge that it has discretion to withhold a point from a teacher where the teacher's performance is deemed to be unsatisfactory. The Governing Body will seek the advice of the LEA before withholding a point for experience in respect of unsatisfactory service.

5. **MANAGEMENT ALLOWANCES**

   There are five levels of management allowances that may be awarded to a teacher who "undertakes significant specified management responsibilities beyond those common to the majority of classroom teachers". This allowance is for a fixed term to 31 March 2005, when responsibilities will be reviewed and finalised in order to assimilate a new management structure in accordance with the School Teachers' Pay and Conditions Document.

   I. The award of management allowances will be linked to clearly defined job descriptions and where allowances are awarded on a temporary basis it will be for a task or a responsibility that is for a limited or specified period. The additional responsibility will be for specific additional weighty responsibilities targeted on Teaching and Learning beyond those common to the majority of classroom teachers.

   II. In the event of a temporary absence of a teacher holding a post which attracts management allowances, the Headteacher may award an acting allowance, in accordance with the Teachers Pay and Conditions Document, where the absence is for a period of more than one half term and the Headteacher requires the duties of the post to be fully carried out.

Doc 12 - Salary policy 2005

The Ugly Face of Institutional Racism

Cardinal Newman School
5th September 2008

Hi Mrs Crow.

Following our brief discussion yesterday afternoon (4th September 2008), I realized there are some discrepancies in the way you calculated my salary or wages. I feel I have been disadvantaged financially by being placed on M3.

(i) I joined Cardinal Newman as an OVERSEAS TRAINED teacher whose qualifications and experience are recognised in England. UK NARIC recognises my qualifications as equivalent to the UK qualifications.

(ii) Like any other overseas trained teacher, I was required to go through a RECOGNITION exercise (QTS), which I completed in June 2008.

(iii) I notice that the school Teachers' Salary Policy Guide which you gave me when you recruited me which I quote below has been abandoned:

SCHOOL TEACHERS' SALARY POLICY (2005)
3 Starting salary of new appointments:
3.1 The Governing Body has adopted the local agreement in respect of the assessment of teachers' pay. The starting salary for all new entrants to the teachers' pay spine without previous teaching or relevant industrial, professional or research experience will be at point M1.
3.2 Where the new entrant to the profession has experience which may count towards salary, points will be awarded as follows:
By reference to paragraph 3 (1) above, plus points in respect of teaching service and industrial, professional and research experience considered to be of value in the performance of the teacher's duties on the basis of 1 point in respect of each complete period of 2 years.

4 Experience
4.1 The Governing Body will award up to six points for experience. A teacher, (including a part time or occasional supply teacher) would be eligible for an experience point for each school year in which the teacher has taught for part of the 26 weeks or was due to but was prevented from doing so for reasons of sickness, maternity or some other absence acknowledged by the Governing Body.

(iv) You wrongly placed me on M3 scale (£24, 048) and yet I have 22 years of teaching experience in Government Schools. I remained in the same grade in which I was when I joined this school (£23,331).

(v) May I remind you that I notice there are inconsistencies in the manner in which you applied this instrument to other colleagues who completed QTS in the past few years who were appropriately placed on M6 because the school took into account their experience before they joined this school. May I point out that the way I have been treated is no different from a newly qualified teacher (NQT).

(iv) I feel that my service has not been valued up to this point. Unless there is a deliberate preferential treatment, there is no justification for awarding a higher salary to people who have less teaching experience than mine.

(vi) I was hoping you were going to invite me for a brief discussion of my new status.

(vii) My greatest fear now is that, as long as I am at Cardinal Newman, I am beginning to accumulate NEW EXPERIENCE. Literally, I am making a new beginning.

(viii) May I urge you to reconsider your position?

Sincerely
Morrison Mwamba Ngwenya.

Doc 15 - Formal complaint

VUPENYU waMWAMBA

RE: Experience

RE: Experience
Morrison Ngwenya
Sent: 16 June 2011 08:22
To: Jane Crow

Hi Jane.
Thanks for the information.
Morrison

From: Jane Crow
Sent: 15 June 2011 15:20
To: Morrison Ngwenya
Cc: Yvonne Pilarski
Subject: RE: Experience

Hi Morrison

Thank you for this information. However, we have to write in the experience from the point of view of when you gained QTS in this country as your previous qualifications were not recognised here. I know it is a bizarre regulation but that is what it is. I am sure when the inspectors are in school you can explain the real background to them.

Jane

From: Morrison Ngwenya
Sent: 15 June 2011 13:09
To: Jane Crow
Cc: Yvonne Pilarski; Jonathan Tucker
Subject: Experience

Hi Jane,

I notice there may be an error in the information provided in the SEF to our visitors and to all members of staff. As you may be aware I was employed as an overseas trained teachers on 1 June 2007. I did not train to become a teacher in the UK. I started teaching in January 1986 which makes my experience more than 4 years. Could you please correct that information and resend so all members of staff so that they have the correct picture of my situation.
Thank You in advance

Morrison

Please consider the environment before printing this email.

Doc 19 - The head teacher's email rejecting my qualifications

Full time teaching staff	Total	81	Cath.	
Part time teaching staff	Total	18	Catholic	7
Support staff	Total	85	Catholic	32

Senior Leadership Team

Name	Responsibilities	Gender	Experience	Current Service	FTE	Catholic Y or N	CCRS/equiv.	NPQH
Jane Crow	Headteacher	F	36	23	1	Y	Y	Y
Fleur Musonda	Deputy Headteacher	F	30	10	1	Y	Y	N
Lucy Whelan	Deputy Headteacher	F	18	9	1	Y	N	N
Lorraine Croft	Assistant Headteacher	F	20	4	1	Y	N	N
Jonathan Tucker	Assistant Headteacher	M	29	20	1	N	N	N
Kendra Slawinski	Assistant Headteacher	F	27	24	1	N	N	N
David Martin	Assistant Headteacher	M	18	8	1	N	N	Y
Gail Hickman	Assistant Headteacher	F	26	13	1	N	N	N
Sue Meader	Business Manager	F	14	3	1	Y	N	N

Staff teaching RE

Name	Responsibilities	QTS	Gender	Experience	Current Service	FTE	Catholic Y/N	CCRS/ equiv.
Sr Yvonne Pilarski	Head of RE Dept	Y	F	35	19	1	Y	Y
Claire Hanefey	Second in RE Dept	Y	F	12	11	1	Y	Y
Morrison Ngwenya	Teacher of RE	Y	M	4	3	1	Y	Y
Patrick Businge	Teacher of RE	Y	M	4	3	1	Y	Y
Lawrence Makokha	Teacher of RE	Y	M	4	2	1	Y	Y
Lidia Kidman	Teacher of RE	Y	F	16	11	1	Y	Y
Karsten Wille	Teacher of RE	Y	M	10	4	1	N	N

[Experience = length of time in teaching; Current Service = time in this school]

COMMENTS: This is the official position of the school namely that they do not accept my qualifications and experience from Overseas.

Doc 21 - Self-Evaluation Form

Secondly you restated the points you made at the disciplinary hearing in that the School had placed you on the incorrect pay point and that this was done on the grounds of your race. However you produced no new evidence to contradict the substantial evidence considered at the disciplinary hearing which showed that the Head teacher, the Local Authority, your own union representative and the Secretary of State for Education did not uphold your complaint in respect of your pay point. You did however admit to us following Mrs Crow's comprehensive explanation of your pay to the Appeal hearing *'that until today'* documents had not pin pointed exactly how you should have been paid.

At the Appeal hearing you referred to information that you had gained regarding the pay points of 20 teachers you had met at a BME conference who were paid at points between M3 and M6. However you refused to provide further details and the Appeal Panel considered that there could have been numerous reasons for their individual rates of pay. Examples of such reasons were provided to the Appeal Panel, including teaching shortage subject areas. You suggested to us that the reason you made the statements about Mrs Crow was that she had said she did not recognise your qualifications. Mrs Crow was clear that this is not what she had said and went on to explain that it is your teaching qualification which is not recognised in this country according to national policies. Mrs Crow was clear that she and the school were following the School Teachers Pay and Conditions Document (STCPD) and said that race had nothing to do with it. You yourself admitted to us at the appeal hearing that you recognise that you did need to achieve QTS. As a panel we were therefore confused why you did not recognise that the reason for your pay point at that time was not purely a judgement made by the Headteacher based on your race.

Regarding the statements you made you confirmed to us that you stood by your statements about Fleur Musonda based on your interpretations of comments she made in a meeting regarding the appointment of a second in department post. However you provided no evidence to suggest that the school did wish to appoint a white candidate to this post.

You also maintained that Sister Yvonne Pilarski 'had an attitude towards you' and suggested that she thought that you were the 'evil one'. The only basis you were able to provide for this view was that she had undertaken joint observations and failed to resolve your pay concerns. You also restated that Kendra had sought to fail you because you were black, again without providing any evidence to this effect.

You suggested to the panel that we needed to understand the background to your statements, however whilst you restated the information described to the hearing panel you put forward no new evidence to support your accusations against staff at the school.

In addition we noted that following the Employment Tribunal proceedings the school asked Mr Garret Fay, Deputy Headteacher, to undertake an internal investigation into your claims of race discrimination and concluded that: "I cannot find any evidence that any of the named parties engaged in any racially or religiously prejudicial activity directed towards Mr Ngwenya." Nor did Mr Fay find that anyone was instructed by Jane Crow to behave in a discriminatory manner.

The original hearing panel had clearly upheld this allegation based on the significant evidence provided to them by documents and witnesses that the statements set out in the allegations were false, inaccurate and misleading. We considered that you provided no further evidence to suggest that your statements were true and accurate. As a result we concluded that we could find no compelling evidence to refute the original hearing panel's conclusion to uphold this allegation. We further do not uphold point 1 of your grounds of appeal as set out above in respect of this allegation.

Doc 22 - Letter from Chair of governors rejecting my qualifications

The Ugly Face of Institutional Racism

Andy Morgan
Chair of Governors
Cardinal Newman School
Warden Hill Road
Luton
27th June 2010

Morrison Ngwenya
29 Acacia Road
Bedford
MK42 OHT

Dear Morrison

Salary Review

Thank you for your email on Tuesday 22 June asking for a formal response from the Governing Body rather than a meeting. I apologise for not responding to you formally in the first instance, but I felt that this situation was better dealt with by a face to face meeting.

I therefore can confirm to you how your salary entitlement has been decided in accordance with our policy.

When you joined Cardinal Newman School your teaching qualifications and previous teaching experience had all been gained abroad and are not fully recognised in this country. You were therefore put on the Unqualified Teacher's Pay Scale. However due to your previous experience the Head Teacher put you at the very top of that scale which at the time was point 10.

In your first year of teaching you attended the necessary course to convert your teaching status to a Qualified Teacher and subsequently at the end of that year you were moved from the Unqualified Teachers Scale onto the Qualified Teachers Pay Scale at point M3 in accordance with the Pay and Conditions Guidance document and the Salary Policy. **You were not entitled to a higher scale as your previous experience was not in one of the institutions listed in the guidance and policy documents and as your teaching experience had,** at the discretion of the head teacher, been taken into account in placing you on scale 10 originally. You will now remain on the Qualified Teacher Pay Scale until you reach M6 at which time you will be entitled to apply to move through the threshold onto the Upper Pay Scale.

Secondly, **CNS is controlled by Luton Borough Council which is a Unitary Authority not a County Council. It may be the case that other schools in Luton are applying their own Pay and Conditions Policies differently to CNS**, but this as at their own discretion as long as they stay with the guidance set out by the Government.

Thirdly, I confirm that I am satisfied that the Salary Policy has been applied to you correctly. I cannot comment on your colleague, but if you ask then to write to me I will look into their case as well.

The Policy Documents that I referred to in previous correspondence are the School Teachers Pay and Conditions Documents, Guidance on School Teachers pay and Conditions published annually by the then DCSF now DofE. The documents provide guidance to Local Authorities and Governing Bodies in

21.1 ANDY MORGAN DOES NOT RECOGNISE origin of qualifications (1)

VUPENYU waMWAMBA

CARDINAL NEWMAN CATHOLIC SCHOOL

A Specialist Science College

Warden Hill Road
Luton
Bedfordshire LU2 7AE
Tel: (01582) 597125
Fax: (01582) 503088
email: Cardinal.Newman.
        Admin@luton.gov.uk

Mr M Ngwenya
29 Acacia Road
BEDFORD
MK42 0HT

5 July 2012

Dear Morrison

SUSPENSION FROM DUTY

I write to confirm the advice given to you in our meeting today.

You are suspended from duty in accordance with Paragraph 5.3 of the school's Disciplinary Procedure, a copy of which I gave you in the meeting. The decision to suspend you has been made as the allegations against you are capable of constituting gross misconduct and it would therefore be inappropriate for you to remain at work during this process.

In November 2011 you issued employment tribunal proceedings against the School in respect of your pay and in which claimed race discrimination and unlawful deductions of wages. The claim was rejected by the employment tribunal on 26th April 2012. During the course of the employment tribunal proceedings, you produced paperwork in which you made various allegations of race discrimination against Jane Crow (headteacher) and other School employees, namely, Fleur Musonda, Jan Piotrowski, Yvonne Pilarski and Kendra Slawinski.

As you know, the School has carried out an investigation into the allegations you raised and could not find any evidence that you were racially discriminated against.

This suspension is therefore to allow the investigation into the allegations that you have committed gross misconduct in that you:

1) Made false, inaccurate or misleading statements;
2) Made vexatious, malicious and/or frivolous complaints; and
3) By carrying out (1) and/or (2) above, there has been an irretrievable loss of trust and confidence between the School and you.

Headteacher Mrs Jane Crow   Deputy Headteachers Mrs Fleur Musonda, Mrs Lucy Whelan, Mr Garret Fay

'Together towards our Lord, through learning, love and faith'

Doc 22.1 - Trumped up charges

The Ugly Face of Institutional Racism

CARDINAL
NEWMAN

CATHOLIC SCHOOL
A Specialist Science College

Mr M M Ngwenya
19 Western Street
Bedford
MK40 1QT

Warden Hill Road
Luton
Bedfordshire LU2 7AE
Tel: (01582) 597 25
Fax: (01582) 503088
email: Cardinal.Newman.
Admin@luton.gov.uk

12 June 2007

Dear Mr Ngwenya

I have pleasure in offering you an appointment as an Overseas Trained Teacher, details of which are set out in the enclosed Statement of Particulars. This Statement of Particulars, together with this letter constitutes your Contract of Employment.

Under the arrangements laid down by the Department for Education and Skills, the appointment of Instructor is permitted provided that no qualified teacher is available to give specialist instruction.

The appointment is subject to:

    a) Confirmation that you hold a recognised qualification. When your qualified teacher status is confirmed you should register with the General Teaching Council.

    b) Confirmation that you hold a valid work permit.

    c) A medical examination which you may be required to undergo at the discretion of the Occupational Health Adviser.

I should be grateful if you would confirm acceptance of the appointment by completing both declarations and returning one to me. All the remaining documents are for your retention.

On taking up your employment, you should forward your Income Tax Form P45, if you had previous employment

If applicable, please send an appropriate notification of opting out of the Teachers' Superannuation Scheme. Please note that, before salary payment can be made to new employees, the enclosed bank credit form must also be completed and returned together with your National Insurance number and, where applicable, a Reduced Rate or Exempt Rate Certificate for National Insurance.

Headteacher
Mrs Jane Crow
Deputy Headteachers
Mr ...
Mr Joe Richardson
Ms Lorraine Croft

Doc 23 - The school creates new contracts to mislead the Employment Tribunal ɔ1

VUPENYU waMWAMBA

CARDINAL NEWMAN

CATHOLIC SCHOOL

A Specialist Science College

Mr M M Ngwenya
19 Western Street
Bedford
MK40 1QT

Warden Hill Road
Luton
Bedfordshire LU2 7AE
Tel: (01582) 597125
Fax: (01582) 503088
email: Cardinal.Newman.Admin@luton.gov.uk

21 August 2007

Dear Mr Ngwenya

I have pleasure in offering you an appointment as an Overseas Trained Teacher, details of which are set out in the enclosed Statement of Particulars. This Statement of Particulars, together with this letter constitutes your Contract of Employment.

Under the arrangements laid down by the Department for Education and Skills, the appointment of Instructor is permitted provided that no qualified teacher is available to give specialist instruction.

The appointment is subject to:

a) Confirmation that you hold a recognised qualification. When your qualified teacher status is confirmed you should register with the General Teaching Council.

b) Confirmation that you hold a valid work permit.

c) A medical examination which you may be required to undergo at the discretion of the Occupational Health Adviser.

I should be grateful if you would confirm acceptance of the appointment by completing both declarations and returning one to me. All the remaining documents are for your retention.

On taking up your employment, you should forward your Income Tax Form P45, if you had previous employment

If applicable, please send an appropriate notification of opting out of the Teachers' Superannuation Scheme. Please note that, before salary payment can be made to new employees, the enclosed bank credit form must also be completed and returned together with your National Insurance number and, where applicable, a Reduced Rate or Exempt Rate Certificate for National Insurance.

Headteacher
Mrs Jane Crow
Deputy Headteachers
Mrs Fleur Musonda
Mr Joe Richardson
Ms Lorraine Croft

'Together towards our Lord, through learning, love and faith w

Doc 23 - The school creates new contracts to mislead the Employment Tribunal p2

The Ugly Face of Institutional Racism

CATHOLIC SCHOOL

A Specialist Science College

Mr Morrison Ngwenya
29 Acacia Road
Bedford
MK42 0HT

Warden Hill Road
Luton
Bedfordshire LU2 7AE
Tel: (01582) 597125
Fax: (01582) 503088
email: Cardinal.Newman
Admin@luton.gov

10 September 2008

Dear Mr Ngwenya,

I have pleasure in offering you a teaching appointment, the details of which are set out in the enclosed Statement of Particulars. This Statement of Particulars, together with this letter, constitutes your Contract of Employment.

The appointment is subject to (where appropriate):

(a) Confirmation by the General Teaching Council for England that you hold Qualified Teacher Status confirming that you possess a recognised teaching qualification and have passed QTS Skills Tests in Literacy, Numeracy and ICT.

(b) Confirmation that you are registered with the General Teaching Council.

(c) A medical examination which you may be required to undergo at the discretion of the Occupational Health Adviser.

(d) A satisfactory Disclosure check in respect of criminal convictions as required by the Police Act 1997 regarding the protection of children.

I should be grateful if you would confirm your acceptance of the appointment by completing both copies of the appointment declaration and returning one copy of each to me at the specified address. All the remaining documents are for your retention.

I wish you well in your employment.

Yours sincerely,

Chair of Governors
Headteacher

Headteacher
Mrs Jane Crow
Deputy Headteachers
Mrs Fleur Musonda
Mr Joe Richardson

Doc 23 - The school creates new contracts to mislead the Employment Tribunal p3

VUPENYU waMWAMBA

CARDINAL NEWMAN SCHOOL

APPOINTMENT DECLARATION – OVERSEAS TRAINED TEACHER

Name: Morrison Mwamba Ngwenya

Post: Teacher

1. I have received the original of this letter and enclosures and accept the appointment on the terms and conditions specified.

2. I have completed an approved course of training and will register with the General Teaching Council when my qualified teacher status is recognised.

3. It will be necessary to collect and process information, collected from yourself and from third parties, relevant to your employment with the school and this Authority. This will include information about your sickness record. In accepting this Statement of Written Particulars **you hereby give your express consent to this**.

Signed: .....*[signature]*...

Date: .....25-th June 2007...

Please return to: Chairperson of Governors at the School

VA12D/01/08

Doc 23 - The school creates new contracts to mislead the Employment Tribunal p4

The Ugly Face of Institutional Racism

CARDINAL NEWMAN SCHOOL

APPOINTMENT DECLARATION – OVERSEAS TRAINED TEACHER

Name: Morrison Mwamba Ngwenya

Post: Teacher

1. I have received the original of this letter and enclosures and accept the appointment on the terms and conditions specified.

2. I have completed an approved course of training and will register with the General Teaching Council when my qualified teacher status is recognised.

3. It will be necessary to collect and process information, collected from yourself and from third parties, relevant to your employment with the school and this Authority. This will include information about your sickness record. In accepting this Statement of Written Particulars **you hereby give your express consent to this**.

Signed: *[signature]*

Date: 25th June 2007

Please return to: Chairperson of Governors at the School

VA12D/01/08

Doc 23 - The school creates new contracts to mislead the Employment Tribunal p5

VUPENYU waMWAMBA

CARDINAL NEWMAN CATHOLIC SCHOOL

APPOINTMENT DECLARATION – OVERSEAS TRAINED TEACHER

Name: Morrison Mwamba Ngwenya

Post: Teacher

1. I have received the original of this letter and enclosures and accept the appointment on the terms and conditions specified.

2. I have completed an approved course of training and will register with the General Teaching Council when my qualified teacher status is recognised.

3. It will be necessary to collect and process information, collected from yourself and from third parties, relevant to your employment with the school and this Authority. This will include information about your sickness record. In accepting this Statement of Written Particulars **you hereby give your express consent to this**.

Signed: *[signature]*

Date: 18/10/07

Please return to: Chairperson of Governors at the School

VA12D/01/08

Doc 23 - The school creates new contracts to mislead the Employment Tribunal p6

The Ugly Face of Institutional Racism

CARDINAL NEWMAN CATHOLIC SCHOOL
APPOINTMENT DECLARATION

Name: Morrison Ngwenya

Post: Teacher of R E

1. I have received the original of this letter and enclosures and accept the appointment on the terms and conditions specified.

2. I have completed, to the satisfaction of the Department for Education and Skills, an approved course of training.

3. It will be necessary to collect and process information, collected from yourself and from third parties, relevant to your employment with the school and this Authority. This will include information about your sickness record. In accepting this Statement of Written Particulars **you hereby give your express consent to this**.

Signed: *[signature]*

Date: 13/10/08

Please return to: Chairperson of Governors at the School

Ref: VA6/01/08

Doc 23 - The school creates new contracts to mislead the Employment Tribunal p7

VUPENYU waMWAMBA

CARDINAL NEWMAN CATHOLIC SCHOOL

EMPLOYMENT RIGHTS ACT 1996

STATEMENT OF PARTICULARS

Name: Morrison Mwamba Ngwenya

Post: Teacher

Grade: Unqualified

Date of Commencement: 1 June 2007

Continuous Employment with the School commenced on:
(if any): 1 June 2007.

Period of Employment:

Your contract of employment is fixed term due to your Unqualified Teacher status in the UK and, unless terminated earlier as provided for below, your employment with the Council will be discharged on 31 July 2008.

The employment of Overseas Teachers is temporary for up to four years while they secure qualified teacher status and will be reviewed at that time subject to the staffing needs of the school and them continuing to hold a valid work permit.

If you are made redundant, periods of service with other employers may be aggregated with your service with the Authority for the purpose of calculating your redundancy payment in accordance with the Redundancy Payment (Local Government) (Modification) Order 1983 as amended. Your continuous service date for this purpose (if any) subject to verification is: 1 June 2007.

1. **TERMS OF EMPLOYMENT**

    Your terms and conditions of employment (including certain provisions relating to your working conditions) are covered by the School Teachers' Pay and Conditions Document, the Education (Teachers) Regulations 1993, Schools Standards and Framework Act 1998, the Articles of Government for the school, the Conditions of Service for School Teachers in England and Wales Canon Law in relation to the governance of the School and by supplementary local collective agreements negotiated with the teachers' union or unions recognised for collective bargaining purposes in respect of the employment group to which you belong. From time to time variations in your terms or conditions of employment will result from negotiations and agreements at national and/or local levels with the recognised union or unions and these will be notified separately or otherwise incorporated in the documents which are available to you for reference. In either instance the effect will be that the changes are

Doc 24 - The school issues several Statements of Particulars to mislead ET p1

The Ugly Face of Institutional Racism

CARDINAL NEWMAN SCHOOL

EMPLOYMENT RIGHTS ACT 1996

STATEMENT OF PARTICULARS

Name: Morrison Mwamba Ngwenya

Post: Teacher

Grade: Unqualified

Date of Commencement: 1 June 2007

Continuous Employment with the School commenced on:
(if any): 1 June 2007.

Period of Employment:

Your contract of employment is fixed term due to the expiry date of your work permit and, unless terminated earlier as provided for below, your employment with the Council will be discharged on 31 July 2008.

The employment of Overseas Teachers is temporary for up to four years while they secure qualified teacher status and will be reviewed at that time subject to the staffing needs of the school and them continuing to hold a valid work permit.

If you are made redundant, periods of service with other employers may be aggregated with your service with the Authority for the purpose of calculating your redundancy payment in accordance with the Redundancy Payment (Local Government) (Modification) Order 1983 as amended. Your continuous service date for this purpose (if any) subject to verification is: 1 June 2007.

1. **TERMS OF EMPLOYMENT**

    Your terms and conditions of employment (including certain provisions relating to your working conditions) are covered by the School Teachers' Pay and Conditions Document, the Education (Teachers) Regulations 1993, Schools Standards and Framework Act 1998, the Articles of Government for the school, the Conditions of Service for School Teachers in England and Wales Canon Law in relation to the governance of the School and by supplementary local collective agreements negotiated with the teachers' union or unions recognised for collective bargaining purposes in respect of the employment group to which you belong. From time to time variations in your terms or conditions of employment will result from negotiations and agreements at national and/or local levels with the recognised union or unions and these will be notified separately or otherwise incorporated in the documents which are available to you for reference. In either instance the effect will be that the changes are

Doc 24 - The school issues several Statements of Particulars to mislead ET p2

VUPENYU waMWAMBA

CARDINAL NEWMAN CATHOLIC SCHOOL
EMPLOYMENT RIGHTS ACT 1996
STATEMENT OF PARTICULARS

Name:	Morrison Mwamba Ngwenya
Post:	Teacher
Grade:	Unqualified
Date of Commencement:	1 June 2007

Continuous Employment with the School on:
(if any): 1 June 2007

Period of Employment:

Your contract of employment is fixed term due to your Unqualified Teacher status in the UK and the expiry of your visa and, unless terminated earlier as provided for below, your employment with the Council will be discharged on 31 July 2008.

The employment of Overseas Teachers is temporary for up to four years while they secure qualified teacher status and will be reviewed at that time subject to the staffing needs of the school and them continuing to hold a valid work permit.

If you are made redundant, periods of service with other employers may be aggregated with your service with the Authority for the purpose of calculating your redundancy payment in accordance with the Redundancy Payment (Local Government) (Modification) Order 1983 as amended. Your continuous service date for this purpose (if any) subject to verification is: 1 June 2007.

1. **TERMS OF EMPLOYMENT**

    Your terms and conditions of employment (including certain provisions relating to your working conditions) are covered by the School Teachers' Pay and Conditions Document, the Education (Teachers) Regulations 1993, Schools Standards and Framework Act 1998, the Articles of Government for the school, the Conditions of Service for School Teachers in England and Wales Canon Law in relation to the governance of the school and by supplementary local collective agreements negotiated with the teachers' union or unions recognised for collective bargaining purposes in respect of the employment group to which you belong. From time to time variations in your terms or conditions of employment will result from negotiations and agreements at national and/or local levels with the recognised union or unions and these will be notified separately or otherwise incorporated in the documents which are available to you for reference. In either instance the effect will be that the changes are

Doc 24 - The school issues several Statements of Particulars to mislead ET p3

CARDINAL NEWMAN CATHOLIC SCHOOL

EMPLOYMENT RIGHTS ACT 1996

STATEMENT OF PARTICULARS

TERMS OF EMPLOYMENT

Your terms and conditions of employment (including certain provisions relating to your working conditions) are covered by the Teachers' Pay and Conditions Document, the Education (Teachers) Regulations 1993, the Schools Standards and Framework Act 1998, the Articles of Government for the school in which you are employed, collective agreements negotiated between the Council of Local Education Authorities and the recognised unions of School Teachers (NEOST) (the Burgundy Book) or of any successor body that may be set up by joint agreement to conduct such negotiations, Canon Law in relation to the governance of the school; and by supplementary local collective agreements negotiated by the LA with the teachers' union or unions recognised by this Council for collective bargaining purposes in respect of the employment group to which you belong. These agreements are contained, respectively, in circulars issued from time to time by NEOST and in other documents including those incorporating decisions made by or on behalf of the Council which are available at your place of work. From time to time variations in your terms or conditions of employment will result from negotiations and agreements at national and/or local levels with the recognised union or unions and these will be notified separately or otherwise incorporated in the documents which are available to you for reference. In either instance the effect will be that the changes are incorporated into your contract of employment.

You are to have regard to the Roman Catholic character of the School and not to do anything in any way detrimental or prejudicial to the interest of the same.

If required, you are to instruct the Holy Scriptures and the Doctrines of the Roman Catholic Church, in accordance with the principles and subject to the discipline thereof to the satisfaction of the Diocesan Religious Inspector or other appointed representatives of the Ordinary, at the time or times appointed for religious instruction, such children as are entrusted entrusted to you and to be present at such religious examinations of the children as may be directed to be held by the Governing Body.

The School undertakes to ensure that changes to the terms set out in this document will be entered into these documents or otherwise notified to you within 28 days of each change.

A copy of the "Conditions of Service for Schoolteachers in England and Wales" (Burgundy Book) is also available for reference at your place of work.

Criminal Records Bureau Check (Disclosure)

Your appointment to this post and ongoing employment is subject to the receipt of a satisfactory Criminal Records Bureau check, known as disclosure. It is the School's final decision as to whether a disclosure is satisfactory or not.

In accepting this offer of employment you agree to be subject to a Criminal Records Bureau check as and when requested. A refusal to comply may result in formal disciplinary action being taken under the Schools Disciplinary Policy and Procedure, which could lead to your dismissal from the school.

Doc 24 - The school issues several Statements of Particulars to mislead ET p4

VUPENYU waMWAMBA

CARDINAL NEWMAN CATHOLIC SCHOOL

EMPLOYMENT RIGHTS ACT 1996

STATEMENT OF PARTICULARS

Name: Morrison Ngwenya

Post: Teacher of R E

Grade: Main Pay Scale

Date of Commencement: 1 August 2008

Continuous Employment with the School (if any): 1 June 2007.

1. If you are made redundant periods of service with other employers may be aggregated with your service with the School for the purpose of calculating your redundancy payment in accordance with the Redundancy Payment (Local Government) (Modification) Order 1983 as amended.

   Your continuous service date for this purpose (if any) subject to verification: 1 june 2007.

2. **TERMS OF EMPLOYMENT**

   Your terms and conditions of employment (including certain provisions relating to your working conditions) are covered by the School Teachers' Pay and Conditions Document, the Education (Teachers) Regulations 1993, Schools Standards and Framework Act 1998, the Articles of Government for the school, the Conditions of Service for School Teachers in England and Wales, Canon Law in relation to the governance of the School and by supplementary local collective agreements negotiated with the teachers' union or unions recognised for collective bargaining purposes in respect of the employment group to which you belong. From time to time variations in your terms or conditions of employment will result from negotiations and agreements at national and/or local levels with the recognised union or unions and these will be notified separately or otherwise incorporated in the documents which are available to you for reference. In either instance the effect will be that the changes are incorporated into your contract of employment.

   You are to have regard to the Roman Catholic character of the School and not to do anything in any way detrimental or prejudicial to the interest of the same.

   If required, you are to instruct the Holy Scriptures and the Doctrines of the Roman

Doc 24 - The school issues several Statements of Particulars to mislead ET p5

The Ugly Face of Institutional Racism

Garret wrote "I cannot find any evidence that any of the named parties engaged in any racially or religiously prejudicial activity directed towards Mr Ngwenya. The interviews seem to suggest that the issues of racial and religious prejudice have come to light following Mr Ngwenys's unsuccessful pay claim. It is also very clear from the investigation that at no time was anyone instructed by the Headteacher to act in a racial or religiously prejudicial towards him. The issue of the named persons working together as organised cabal intent on undermining him also seems to be without basis. The strategies introduced by the named persons interviewed all suggest that they each acted in good faith and in a manner designed to support Mr Ngwenya's professional development".

Garret confirmed when interviewed that he had never witnessed a staff member being racist towards another staff member.

Jane stated "there is no place for racism in Christianity and the way I act. We work very hard in school to ensure racism is stamped out and would not accept it in the way staff are towards each other, Morrison's comments are so unjustified.....We have a diverse mix of students at Cardinal Newman Secondary School. It is unthinkable that staff or parents think we operate like this. I have spent a lot of time calming and managing staff who have been upset by his allegations" and "Morrison has never had a conversation with me to do with his pay that mentioned undue stress applied by other members of staff or racial discrimination".

Jane further stated "Although he understands he is an Overseas Trained Teacher (OTT), in his mind there is a misunderstanding that although we fully accept his degree and other qualifications are valid and authenticated by NARIC, we cannot accept the teaching qualifications of those trained outside the EEA".

Fleur stated "He never mentioned any of this at the time and these things have only come to light since the end of last year. I feel he is trying to prove a different matter and get compensation and does not care who he attacks in the process. With regard to the meeting in the RE office, the office is really small and was very crowded and I only turned round to Ashley to show her she was part of the meeting. It is complete nonsense to say it was because she is white".

Jan stated "I have not witnessed staff being racist towards Morrison".

Jonathan stated "I have worked here for 22 years and on the whole the working relationships at the school are very good. There is a strong relationship between the staff members and it is a happy place to work" and "Jane has never referred to his ethnicity re his profession and salary calculated at the school. Mr Ngwenya is completely misrepresenting Mrs Crow when he alleges that she is a racist" and "Mr Ngwenya has also inferred that Mrs Musonda, Mrs Slawinski, Mr Piotrowski and Sister Yvonne had had a campaign against him. This is totally untrue. It is untrue re his race and ethnicity and it is insulting. He sometimes makes ill-judged remarks to students and has poor classroom control. These reports have been made to him in a professional manner and regards his capability".

Doc 25 - Body of governors quotes the head teacher rejecting qualifications

VUPENYU waMWAMBA

CARDINAL NEWMAN CATHOLIC SCHOOL

A Specialist Science College

18 February 2013

Mr M Ngwenya
29 Acacia Road
BEDFORD
MK42 0HT

Warden Hill Road
Luton
Bedfordshire LU2 7AE
Tel: (01582) 597125
Fax: (01582) 503088
email: Cardinal.Newman.
Admin@luton.gov.uk

Dear Mr Ngwenya

Thank you for your letter dated 11 February 2013 regarding the notification of the appeal hearing. I acknowledge your confirmation that you are able to attend on that date.

The appeal hearing that will take place on the 5 March 2013 is your right of appeal to the Governing Body against the decision of the disciplinary hearing panel regarding disciplinary action taken against you. As previously stated the appeal panel is only able to consider those points in your letter of appeal dated 22 January 2013 that comply with section 7.1:2 of the disciplinary procedure. For clarity, I refer you to the points at 7.1.2 set out below, regarding your grounds of appeal:

- it is against the findings that the allegations have been substantiated and/or against the form of disciplinary action taken

- the disciplinary procedure has been applied defectively or unfairly

- new evidence has come to light which was not available at the disciplinary hearing and which may make a difference to the original decision.

Whilst helpful for the panel to be aware of the issues you wish to raise at the appeal hearing, I must remind you that if the points you raise are not relevant to the disciplinary procedure it will be my role as Chair of the Panel to ensure that the proceedings deal with the relevant points as set out above. For the avoidance of doubt and to assist you in the preparation of your appeal I would stress that we are not going to hear any more arguments from you regarding your salary.

You have for over 5 years now been advised by everyone that you have consulted that the decisions taken by the school regarding your salary were correct. You have exhausted all avenues of appeal that the Governors have any jurisdiction over with regard to this matter and therefore this appeal panel will not consider any further points on this.

I would therefore recommend that your carefully consider the points you wish to raise in relation to findings of the disciplinary hearing and that your appeal be based on these.

Continued ....

Headteacher Mrs Jane Crow   Deputy Headteachers Mrs Fleur Musonda, Mrs Lucy Whelan, Mr Garret Fay

'Together towards our Lord, through learning, love and faith'

Doc 26 - Chair of governor's takes a defiant position p1

The Ugly Face of Institutional Racism

CARDINAL NEWMAN

CATHOLIC SCHOOL

A Specialist Science College

Warden Hill Road
Luton
Bedfordshire LL2 7AE

Tel: (01582) 597125
Fax: (01582) 503088
email: Cardinal.Newman.
Admin@luton.gov.uk

May 2008

To whom it may concern

Morrison Ngwenya has been a member of the RE Department in Cardinal Newman School for the past two years. During that time, I have found him to be a very pleasant and hard-working colleague. He has a good sense of humour which is an asset in such a demanding job! He has a very good working relationship with all the members of the department and is always willing to share his time and resources and keen to learn from more experienced colleagues.

Morrison has a very sound and secure knowledge and understanding of the requirements of the Religious Education curriculum.

He was an experienced teacher in his home country of Zimbabwe. Since coming to the UK he has worked hard, and indeed is still working hard, to understand the challenges of teaching RE in a large Catholic comprehensive in Great Britain, where teaching methods and the attitudes of students towards learning are very different from those in place previously.

I really admire him for the way he is coming to terms with the differences and for his application to providing high quality lessons which will motivate and engage the students.

Morrison has high expectations of his students, both in terms of behaviour and academic achievement. He works hard to build up positive relationships in the classroom and immediately seeks help and support should difficulties arise. Morrison assiduously plans his lessons, marks his books and assesses the students according to the school and department assessment policy. He is not afraid of spending time in this area to ensure he gives the best he can to his students. He is quickly learning different teaching methods which can be used to motivate even the most difficult of students.

I have no doubt that Morrison will benefit greatly from the Qualified Teacher Status programme and all that he learns will contribute to him becoming a first class teacher.

Sr Yvonne Pilarski

Sister Yvonne Pilarski
Head of RE

'Together towards our Lord, through learning, love and faith'

Headteacher
Mrs Jane Crow
Deputy Headteachers
Mrs Fleur Musonda
Mr Joe Richardson
Ms Lorraine Croft

Doc 26 - Chair of governor's takes a defiant position p2

VUPENYU waMWAMBA

Contact: Fiona Hutton	**Human Resources**
Direct line: 01582 548051	Apex House
Email:	30-34 Upper George Street
Our ref:	Luton LU1 2RD
Your ref:	
www.luton.gov.uk	Tel: 01582 54 60 00
	Fax: 01582 54 63 50

Personal and confidential
Mr M Ngwenya
29 Acacia Road
Bedford
MK42 0HT

INVESTOR IN PEOPLE

20 August 2012

Dear Mr Ngwenya,

I write with reference to your letter dated 9 August 2012.

Please be advised that your grievance that Cardinal Newman School will now be investigating will be your claim that you have experienced 'differential treatment' as a result of your submission to the Employment Tribunal and subsequent Tribunal Hearing in April 2012. Your letter of 9 August suggests that you may expect the matter of 'breach of contract' to be re-investigated when this has already been subject to a previous investigation by the school and to the scrutiny of the Employment Tribunal which found in the School's favour. This matter will not be revisited.

I am not in possession of the letter which suspended you to which you refer. It is normal practice for such a letter to outline the allegations which will be investigated. (These allegations can change during the course of an investigation). However, these will remain **allegations** until the conclusion of the disciplinary process. The outcome of the investigation can be include 'no disciplinary case to answer' (and no further action taken) through to a formal disciplinary hearing being convened. It is not therefore the case that 'investigations are just a formality' as you assert. There has been no determination on the outcome of the investigation.

In addition I note, in your penultimate paragraph, you state that the 'ACAS disciplinary procedure has been violated'. Please be advised that, should you have any issues about how the School's disciplinary procedure has been applied you should raise these as part of the disciplinary process.

As previously advised, the School will appoint a suitable Governor to investigate your grievance and s/he will be in contact with you early in the new term with details of how the investigation will be taken forward.

Yours sincerely

Fiona Hutton

Fiona Hutton
HR Team Manager (Schools and Traded Services)

CUSTOMER & CORPORATE SERVICES
Corporate Director: Steve Heappey

LUTON BOROUGH COUNCIL

Doc 28 - HR supports the head teacher

The Ugly Face of Institutional Racism

EMPLOYMENT TRIBUNALS

To: Jasbir Josen
Legal Services
Luton Borough Council
Town Hall
George Street
Luton
Beds
LU1 2BQ

Huntingdon Law Courts, Walden Road,
Huntingdon, Cambridgeshire, PE29 3DW

Office 01480 415600
Fax 01480 415620
96650 Huntingdon 2

e-mail:HuntingdonET@hmcts.gsi.gov.uk

To: Mr M Ngwenya
29 Acacia Road
Bedford
MK42 0HT

Case Number 3400484/2013, 3400654/2013, 3400722/2013

Claimant		Respondent
Mr M Ngwenya	V	Cardinal Newman Catholic Secondary School

NOTICE OF PRE-HEARING REVIEW
Employment Tribunals Rules of Procedure 2004

An Employment Judge will conduct a Pre-Hearing Review ('PHR') at *Employment Tribunals, 8-10 Howard Street, Bedford, Beds, MK40 3HS,* commencing on *Friday, 21 June 2013* at *10:00 am* or as soon thereafter on that day as the Tribunal can hear it. [The Tribunal may transfer your case at short notice to be heard at another hearing centre within the region.] It has been given a time allocation of *3 hours.* If you think that is not long enough, you must give your reasons, in writing, together with your time estimate by 17 June 2013.

The matters to be clarified and, if appropriate, decided at the PHR are:

To hear the Respondent's application to strike out or for a deposit order on the ground that the claims have no or little prospect of success.

You may submit written representations for consideration at the hearing. If so, they must be sent to the tribunal and to all other parties not less than 7 days before the hearing. You will have the chance to put forward oral arguments in any case.

A copy of the booklet 'The hearing' (and expenses leaflet if applicable) can be found on our website at
www.justice.gov.uk/tribunals/employment/claims/booklets

A location map for the office can be found at
www.justice.gov.uk/tribunals/employment/venues

10 ET4.PHR   10.5

Doc 29 - Employment Tribunal distracts the processes p1

VUPENYU waMWAMBA

EMPLOYMENT TRIBUNALS

To:	Mr M Ngwenya 29 Acacia Road Bedford Bedfordshire MK42 0HT	8-10 Howard Street, Bedford, MK40 3HS Office :01234 351306 Fax 01234 352315
To	Jasbir Josen Luton Borough Council Legal Services Town Hall Luton LU1 2BQ	e-mail:BedfordET@Tribunals.gsi.gov.uk

Case Number 1201670/2011

Claimant		Respondent
Mr M Ngwenya	V	Cardinal Newman Secondary School Mrs Jane Crow

NOTICE OF CASE MANAGEMENT DISCUSSION
Employment Tribunals Rules of Procedure 2004

A Case Management Discussion ('CMD') will be conducted by an Employment Judge at **Employment Tribunals, 8 -10 Howard Street, Bedford, Bedfordshire,** commencing on **Friday, 9 March 2012** at **02:00 pm** or as soon thereafter on that day as the Tribunal can hear it. [The Tribunal may transfer your case at short notice to be heard at another hearing centre within the region.] It has been given a time allocation of **2.5 hours**.

Please ensure that you attend so that the discussion can start on time.

CMD

You must be able to discuss:

- **To identify and resolve any outstanding case management issues**

A copy of the booklet 'The hearing' and expenses leaflet can be found on our website at www.employmenttribunals.gov.uk/Publications/publications.htm

A location map for the office can be found at
www.employmenttribunals.gov.uk/HearingCentres/hearingCentres.htm

Doc 29 - Employment Tribunal distracts the processes p2

The Ugly Face of Institutional Racism

EMPLOYMENT TRIBUNALS

To: Mr M Ngwenya
29 Acacia Road
Bedford
Bedfordshire
MK42 0HT

Huntingdon Law Courts, Walden Road,
Huntingdon, Cambridgeshire, PE29 3DW

Office : 01480 415800
96650 Huntingdon 2

e-mail: HuntingdonET@hmcts.gsi.gov.uk

Your Ref:
Date   01 October 2013
Case Number: 3400484/2013

Claimant   **Respondent**
Mr M Ngwenya   v   Cardinal Newman Catholic
                                                         Secondary School

Dear Sir / Madam,

ACKNOWLEDGMENT OF CORRESPONDENCE
Employment Tribunals Rules of Procedure 2013

Employment Judge Moore has directed me to write to you with the following.

The Tribunal does not try cases in correspondence. A preliminary hearing has been listed and these issues may be raised then.

The preliminary hearing will be open and I will consider striking out either party for non compliance with orders.

Yours faithfully,

DEKPOFFIONG
For the Tribunal Office

cc   Jasbir Josen
     Legal Services
     Luton Borough Council
     Town Hall
     George Street
     Luton
13.3C Ack and copy – claimant

Doc 29 - Employment Tribunal distracts the processes p3

VUPENYU waMWAMBA

EMPLOYMENT TRIBUNALS

To: Mr M Ngwenya
29 Acacia Road
Bedford
Bedfordshire
MK42 0HT

Huntingdon Law Courts, Walden Road,
Huntingdon, Cambridgeshire, PE29 3DW

Office : 01480 415600
96650 Huntingdon 2

e-mail: HuntingdonET@hmcts.gsi.gov.uk

Your Ref:
Date   29 August 2013
Case Number: 3400484/2013

Claimant   **Respondent**
Mr M Ngwenya   v   Cardinal Newman Catholic
                                                          Secondary School

Dear Sir / Madam,

ACKNOWLEDGMENT OF CORRESPONDENCE
Employment Tribunals Rules of Procedure 2013

I refer to your letter dated 16th August 2013 and 23rd August 2013 which has been placed on the file.
Employment Judge Moore has directed as follows, the issues can be raised at the outset of the hearing.
I am copying this letter as indicated below.

Yours faithfully,

DYLAN BEYEA
For the Tribunal Office

cc   Jasbir Josen
      Legal Services
      Luton Borough Council
      Town Hall
      George Street
      Luton
      Beds
      LU1 2BQ

13.3C Ack and copy – claimant

Doc 29 - Employment Tribunal distracts the processes p4

The Ugly Face of Institutional Racism

EMPLOYMENT TRIBUNALS

To: Mr M Ngwenya
29 Acacia Road
Bedford
MK42 0HT

Huntingdon Law Courts, Walden Road,
Huntingdon, Cambridgeshire, PE29 3DW

To: Jasbir Josen
Legal Services
Luton Borough Council
Town Hall
Luton
LU1 2BQ

Office :01480 415600
Fax 01480 415620
96650 Huntingdon 2

e-mail:HuntingdonET@hmcts.gsi.gov.uk

Case Number 3400484/2013

Claimant		Respondent
Mr M Ngwenya	v	Cardinal Newman Catholic Secondary School

NOTICE OF PRELIMINARY HEARING
CASE MANAGEMENT
Employment Tribunals Rules of Procedure 2013

An Employment Judge will conduct a preliminary hearing to make case management orders including orders relating to the conduct of the final hearing.

The hearing will take place at **Employment Tribunals, 8-10 Howard Street, Bedford, Beds, MK40 3HS,** on **Friday, 11 October 2013** at **10:00 am**, in private. It has been given a time allocation of **2 hours**. If you feel that this is insufficient, please inform us in writing within 7 days of the date of this letter.

Please ensure that you attend so that the discussion can start on time.

Unless there are exceptional circumstances, no application for a postponement will be granted. Any such application must be in writing.

The purpose of the preliminary hearing is:

To clarify any outstanding issues.

Signed,

MRS S JACKSON
For the Tribunal Office

Date : 25 September 2013

7.7 Preliminary hearing – notice of case management discussion - both parties -Rule 53 & 54

Doc 29 - Employment Tribunal distracts the processes p5

VUPENYU waMWAMBA

EMPLOYMENT TRIBUNALS

To: Mr M Ngwenya
29 Acacia Road
Bedford
Bedfordshire
MK42 0HT

Huntingdon Law Courts, Walden Road,
Huntingdon, Cambridgeshire, PE29 3DW

Office : 01480 415600
96650 Huntingdon 2

e-mail: HuntingdonET@hmcts.gsi.gov.uk

Your Ref:
Date   29 August 2013
Case Number: 3400484/2013

Claimant   **Respondent**
Mr M Ngwenya   v   Cardinal Newman Catholic
                                                        Secondary School

Dear Sir / Madam,

ACKNOWLEDGMENT OF CORRESPONDENCE
Employment Tribunals Rules of Procedure 2013

I refer to your letter dated 16th August 2013 and 23rd August 2013 which has been placed on the file.
Employment Judge Moore has directed as follows, the issues can be raised at the outset of the hearing.
I am copying this letter as indicated below.

Yours faithfully,

DYLAN BEYEA
For the Tribunal Office

cc   Jasbir Josen
     Legal Services
     Luton Borough Council
     Town Hall
     George Street
     Luton
     Beds
     LU1 2BQ

13.3C Ack and copy – claimant

Doc 29 - Employment Tribunal distracts the processes p6

The Ugly Face of Institutional Racism

Case Number: 1201670/2011

EMPLOYMENT TRIBUNALS

Claimant Mr M Ngwenya

Respondent Cardinal Newman Secondary School Mrs Jane Crow

HEARD AT: BEDFORD **ON:** 9 March 2012

BEFORE: Employment Judge Adamson

REPRESENTATION

For the Claimant: In person

For the Respondent: Mr J Josen (Solicitor)

CASE MANAGEMENT DISCUSSION

1. This hearing was called to deal with Case Management issues that were arising between the parties.

2. The Claimant is a teacher who qualified, initially overseas, obtained qualifications overseas and has subsequently worked in this country. The Claimant worked at Mark Rutherford School in Bedford until he gained new employment with the Respondent in 2007. There is no dispute that the Claimant's employer is Cardinal Newman Secondary School, the Claimant confirming that to me on two occasions. The Claimant's position is that the Respondent began to discriminate him when he gained qualified teacher status and was placed on scale and point M3 in July 2008 (although he later informed me that he was not paid at this scale until 2009). The Claimant further informed me that the pay for scale and point M3 is the same as for the top of the unqualified teacher scale being the pay he was earning before he gained qualified teacher status and incidentally the rate that he was paid at Mark Rutherford School.

3. The Claimant informed me that following the Respondent placing him at M3 the Respondent required him to undergo an induction which was unnecessary and

VUPENYU waMWAMBA

Case Number: 1201670/2011

which induction was carried out contrary to government guidance. The Claimant's position is that the Respondent imposed the induction on him with the intention that he would fail it, but that he did not, and because he did not he did not receive any feedback from the University. The Claimant further informed that there were considerably more observations than were necessary during that induction and that during some of those observations two teachers observed rather than one so that one could be a witness for the other. The Claimant passed his induction at the end of the academic year 2008/2009.

4. The Claimant has continued to be paid on the Main pay scale but has now reached the top. Having reached the top the Claimant, so he informed me, must be at that level for two years and then can be recommended to move on to the upper pay scale. The Claimant's position is that in accordance with what he describes as a statutory instrument which deals with overseas qualifications and experience he should have been placed at M6 in 2008, but was not, so placed on the ground of his race. The Claimant describes his race as Black African and his case is that if he had been any other race he would, at that time, have been placed at M6. This is the basis of the compensation the Claimant seeks for loss of earnings in his direct race discrimination complaint and in his complaint of unauthorised deduction from wages.

5. Although the Claimant considers that he was discriminated against in respect of the induction process that is not part of the claim made to the tribunal. The Claimant informed me that the Head teacher of the Respondent's School and the Respondent refused to change his grade in 2009, that also is not part of the claim before the tribunal. Since that time the Claimant says he has been acting in accordance with a "protocol" dealing with Luton Borough Council and the Secretary of State. The details of the communications between the Claimant and Luton Borough Council and the Secretary of State were not made known today.

6. In addition to loss of earnings in the discrimination complaint the Claimant also seeks damages for injury to feelings and personal injury. The Claimant has prepared a schedule of loss. In respect of that matter and indeed the claim generally I reminded the Claimant it was for him to establish the remedy he sought.

7. There is one complaint of race discrimination only before the tribunal, namely direct discrimination, the less favourable treatment alleged being or on the ground of race the Respondent placed the Claimant on scale M3 in July (or it may have been August or September) 2008. Apart from remedy the issues in that complaint are:
   1) whether the Respondent's employment of the Claimant on scale M3 when it did in 2008 was on the ground of the Claimant's race; and
   2) whether the tribunal has jurisdiction to consider that complaint, having regard to the relevant time limit for presentation of such complaints and the date the claim was presented to the Tribunal. (There is no dispute that if the tribunal does have jurisdiction and the Respondent acted less favourable as alleged it was to the Claimant's detriment).

8. The issue in the complaint of unauthorised deduction from wages is whether the wages properly payable to the Claimant on being appointed on scale and point M3, as subsequently increased by annual increments have been paid or whether

Doc 29 - Employment Tribunal distracts the processes p8

Case Number: 1201670/2011

the wages properly payable was at M6 of the main scale and then at a higher grade. In this matter there is also a dispute as to whether the Claimant ever entered into an agreement in 2008, or other type, to be employed at grade and point M3.

9. There has been, it would appear, unhappy communication between the parties' over disclosure of document's, the Respondent's position being that the Claimant having informed that he had document's in his control but would not provide copies to the Respondent when it requested. Today, before me the Claimant handed a bundle of document's to the Respondent and informed that they were all the outstanding documents. It must be noted that wages 'properly payable' means the wages that the Respondent was contractually obliged to pay, not what a party considers the Respondent ought to have paid.

10. The parties are in dispute about the presentation of the bundle. I reminded the parties that one bundle was to be made, the contents of which should be indexed paginated and in chronological order. I further informed that neither party had veto of the contents of the bundle.

11. The extent of the claim and the issues having being clarified the Hearing will be expected to conclude within the time allocated. It may well be that the tribunal hearing the claim will consider dealing with the issue of whether it has jurisdiction to consider the claim because of the date the claim was presented and the relevant time limits before hearing any evidence on the merits of the claim, but that is a matter for that tribunal.

12. The Respondent reminded the Claimant that it considers the claim to be misconceived and has put him on notice of its intention to seek costs should the claim be unsuccessful.

ORDERS

1. Case Management Order 4 made on 30th December 2011 (i.e. exchange of witness statements) is varied by the deletion of "2nd March 2012" in the first line of that order and the substitution therefore with "8th April 2012".

Employment Judge, Bedford

ORDER SENT TO THE PARTIES ON
March 2012
FOR THE SECRETARY TO THE TRIBUNALS

Doc 29 - Employment Tribunal distracts the processes p9

VUPENYU waMWAMBA

EMPLOYMENT TRIBUNALS

To: Jasbir Josen
Luton Borough Council
D X 5926 Luton

8-10 Howard Street, Bedford, MK40 3HS

Office : 01234 351306
Fax: 01234 352315

e-mail: BedfordET@hmcts.gsi.gov.uk

Date   06 March 2012
Case Number: 1201670/2011

Claimant		Respondent
Mr M Ngwenya	V	Cardinal Newman Secondary School Mrs Jane Crow

Dear Sir / Madam,

ACKNOWLEDGEMENT OF CORRESPONDENCE
Employment Tribunals Rules of Procedure 2004

I refer to your letter dated 24/02/2012, which has been placed on the file. Employment Judge Moore has directed that the issue of varying orders can be raised at the Case Management Discussion listed on 09/03/2012.

Yours faithfully,

SONIA RAI
For the Secretary of Employment Tribunals

cc   Mr M Ngwenya
29 Acacia Road
Bedford
Bedfordshire
MK42 0HT

Acas – East

150-R Acknowledgement of correspondence – respondent   1.1 R

Doc 29 - Employment Tribunal distracts the processes p10

The Ugly Face of Institutional Racism

1 Your details

1.1	Title:		Mr ✓	Mrs	Miss	Ms	Other
1.2*	First name (or names):		Morrison				
1.3*	Surname or family name:		Ngwenya				
1.4	Date of birth (date/month/year):		26/12/1962	Are you: male?	✓ female?		
1.5*	Address:	Number or Name	29				
		Street	Acacia Road				
	+	Town/City	Bedford				
		County	Bedfordshire				
		Postcode	MK42 0HT				
1.6	Phone number including area code (where we can contact you in the day time):		01234 342 649				
	Mobile number (if different):		07791135378				
1.7	How would you prefer us to communicate with you? (Please tick only one box)		E-mail ✓	Post			
	E-mail address:		morrisonngwenya@yahoo.co.uk				

2 Respondent's details

2.1*	Give the name of your employer or the organisation you are claiming against.		Mrs Jane Crow
			Cardinal Newman Secondary School
2.2*	Address:	Number or Name	Warden Hill Road
		Street	Warden Hill Road
	+	Town/City	Luton
		County	Bedfordshire
		Postcode	LU2 7AE
	Phone number:		01582597125
2.3	If you worked at a different address from the one you have given at 2.2, please give the full address and postcode.		
	Postcode		
	Phone number:		

If there are other respondents please complete **Section 11.**

ET1 v03 001

Doc 32 - ET1 Claim of race discrimination p1

VUPENYU waMWAMBA

3 Employment details

3.1 Please give the following information if possible.

When did your employment start? 01/06/2007

Is your employment continuing? Yes ✓ No

If your employment has ceased, or you are in a period of notice, when did it, or will it, end?

3.2 Please say what job you do or did. Teacher

4 Earnings and benefits

4.1 How many hours on average do, or did, you work each week? 37 hours each week

4.2 How much are, or were, you paid?

Pay before tax £ 2237.00 Hourly
Normal take-home pay (including overtime, commission, bonuses and so on) £ 1621.00
Weekly
Monthly ✓
Yearly

4.3 If your employment has ended, did you work (or were you paid for) a period of notice? Yes No

If 'Yes', how many weeks' or months' notice did you work, or were you paid for? weeks months

4.4 Were you in your employer's pension scheme? Yes ✓ No

Please answer 4.5 to 4.9 if your claim, or part of it, is about unfair or constructive dismissal.

4.5 If you received any other benefits, e.g. company car, medical insurance, etc, from your employer, please give details.

N/A

4.6 Since leaving your employment have you got another job? Yes No
If 'No', please now go straight to section 4.9.

4.7 Please say when you started (or will start) work.

Doc 32 - ET1 Claim of race discrimination p2

The Ugly Face of Institutional Racism

4.8 Please say how much you are now earning (or will earn). £ [   ] .00 each [   ]

4.9 Please tick the box to say what you want if your case is successful:

    a To get your old job back and compensation (reinstatement)

    b To get another job with the same employer and compensation (re-engagement)

    c Compensation only

5 Your claim

5.1* Please tick one or more of the boxes below. In the space provided, describe the event, or series of events, that have caused you to make this claim:

    a I was unfairly dismissed (including constructive dismissal)

    b I was discriminated against on the grounds of

Sex (including equal pay)	Race ✓
Disability	Religion or belief
Sexual orientation	Age

    c I am claiming a redundancy payment

    d I am owed   notice pay
                          holiday pay
                          arrears of pay ✓
                          other payments

    e Other complaints

5.2* Please set out the background and details of your claim in the space below. The details of your claim should include **the date when the event(s) you are complaining about happened**; for example, if your claim relates to discrimination give the dates of all the incidents you are complaining about, or at least the date of the last incident. If your complaint is about payments you are owed please give the dates of the period covered. Please use the blank sheet at the end of the form if needed.

Salary discrimination.
Following our brief discussion yesterday afternoon (4th September 2008), I realized there are some discrepancies in the way you calculated my salary or wages. I feel I have been disadvantaged financially by being placed on M3.
(i) I joined Cardinal Newman as an OVERSEAS TRAINED teacher whose qualifications and experience are recognised in England. UK NARIC recognises my qualifications as equivalent to the UK qualifications.
(ii) Like any other overseas trained teacher, I was required to go through a RECOGNITION exercise (QTS) which I completed in June 2008.
(iii) I notice that the school Teachers' Salary Policy Guide which you gave me when you recruited me which I quote below has been abandoned:
SCHOOL TEACHERS' SALARY POLICY (2005)
3 Starting salary of new appointments:
3.1 The Governing Body has adopted the local agreement in respect of the assessment of teachers' pay.

ET1 v03 003   3   ET1 v03 003

Doc 32 - ET1 Claim of race discrimination p3

The starting salary for all new entrants to the teachers' pay spine without previous teaching or relevant industrial, professional or research experience will be at point M1.
3.2 Where the new entrant to the profession has experience which may count towards salary, points will be awarded as follows:
By reference to paragraph 3 (1) above, plus points in respect of teaching service and industrial, professional and research experience considered to be of value in the performance of the teacher's duties on the basis of 1 point in respect of each complete period of 2 years.
4 Experience
4.1 The Governing Body will award up to six points for experience. A teacher, (including a part time or occasional supply teacher) would be eligible for an experience point for each school year in which the teacher has taught for part of the 26 weeks or was due to but was prevented from doing so for reasons of sickness, maternity or some other absence acknowledged by the Governing Body.
(iv) You wrongly placed me on M3 scale (£24, 048) and yet I have 22 years of teaching experience in Government Schools. I remained in the same grade in which I was when I joined this school (£23,331).
(v) May I remind you that I notice there are inconsistencies in the manner in which you applied this instrument to other colleagues who completed QTS in the past few years who were appropriately placed on M6 because the school took into account their experience before they joined this school. May I point out that the way I have been treated is no different from a newly qualified teacher (NQT).
I am appealing to the Employment Tribunal for loss of remunerations because the school:
• failed to apply the provisions of the STPCD 2008 correctly
• failed to take account of relevant evidence
• failed to have proper regard for statutory guidance
• took account of irrelevant or inaccurate evidence, were biased or discriminated against me.

5.3 If your claim consists of, or includes, a claim that you are making a protected disclosure under the Employment Rights Act 1996 (otherwise known as a 'whistleblowing' claim), please tick the box below if you wish a copy of this form, or information from it, to be forwarded on your behalf to a relevant regulator (known as a 'prescribed person' under the relevant legislation) by the Tribunals Service.

6 What compensation or remedy are you seeking?

6.1 Completion of this section is optional, but may help if you state what compensation or remedy you are seeking from your employer as a result of this complaint. If you specify an amount, please explain how you have calculated that figure.

The school should re-instate my salary to M6 (£29427) as at July 2008 when I passed QTS. This salary should apply for ONE years (2008/2009. In 2009/201-2010/2011, I should have been at UPS1.
Normally one should have been in M6 for one (1) only there after move on to UPS 1.
Salary areas for 2008/2009 should be £29427-£24048 = £5379.
Salary for 2009 ; 2010; 2011 would then be adjusted accordingly against UPS1 which is about £34 000.

7 Other information

7.1 Please do not send a covering letter with this form. You should add any extra information you want us to know here. Please use the blank sheet at the end of the form if needed.

8 Your representative

Please fill in this section only if you have appointed a representative. If you do fill in this section, we will in future only send correspondence to your representative and not to you.

8.1 Representative's name: N/A

8.2 Name of the representative's organisation:

8.3 Address:
- Number or Name
- Street
- Town/City
- County
- Postcode

8.4 Phone number (including area code):

Mobile number (if different):

8.5 Reference:

8.6 How would they prefer us to communicate with them? E-mail ☐ Post ☐
(Please tick only one box)

E-mail address:

9 Disability

9.1 Please tick this box if you consider you have a disability Yes ☐
Please say what this disability is and tell us what assistance, if any, you will need as your claim progresses through the system, including for any hearings that may need to be held at Tribunal Service premises.

N/A

10 Multiple cases

10.1 To your knowledge, is your claim one of a number of claims against Yes ☐ No ☐
the same employer arising from the same, or similar, circumstances?

Doc 32 - ET1 Claim of race discrimination p5

VUPENYU waMWAMBA

11 Details of Additional Respondents

- Name of your employer or the organisation you are claiming against. — N/A
- Address:
  - Number or Name
  - Street
  - + Town/City
  - County
  - Postcode
- Phone number:

- Name of your employer or the organisation you are claiming against.
- Address:
  - Number or Name
  - Street
  - + Town/City
  - County
  - Postcode
- Phone number:

- Name of your employer or the organisation you are claiming against.
- Address:
  - Number or Name
  - Street
  - + Town/City
  - County
  - Postcode
- Phone number:

Please read the form and check you have entered all the relevant information. Once you are satisfied, please tick this box. ✓

Data Protection Act 1998. We will send a copy of this form to the respondent(s) and Acas. We will, if your claim consists of, or includes, a claim that you have made a protected disclosure under the Employment Rights Act 1996 (and you have given your consent that we should do so) send a copy of the form, or extracts from it, to the relevant regulator. We will put the information you give us on this form onto a computer. This helps us to monitor progress and produce statistics. Information provided on this form is passed to the Department for Business, Innovation and Skills to assist research into the use and effectiveness of employment tribunals.

ET1 v03 006

Doc 32 - ET1 Claim of race discrimination p6

Additional information for sections 5.2 and 7.
UNLAWFUL DISCRIMINATION IN WARDING SALARY.
I completed teacher training in Zimbabwe in 1985 and started teaching in January 1986. Ever since that year I have never earned a living outside teaching. When I came over to the UK, I sent my qualifications to NARIC for valuation or verification. My qualifications were rated as equivalent to the UK qualifications. I immediately enrolled for QTS which I completed in 2008. After completing QTS my salary did not change as I hoped it would after completing QTS. Among the reasons I was given by the Head teacher in the several appeals I made with her include the following:
(i) The very first response the Head teacher gave me in 2008 was: 'complete your QTS then we will see your so-called qualifications and experience'
(ii) Next the Head also allayed my fears when she assured me that I had residuals following my GCSE classes who had passed with 'As' and 'Bs'.
(iii) Next the Head said 'the school cannot recognise your overseas qualifications and experience',
(iv) The next was, your performance is still at 'satisfactory' so we cannot grade you to M6,
(v) When I kept pressing I was informed: After all the school has no money.
(vi) And finally 'You will still get to M6 anyway.'
I felt the school was in breach of the School Teachers' Pay and Conditions Document (STPCD) 2009, paragraphs 18.1.1 and 37.1), and that of Cardinal Newman School Teachers' Salary Policy (2005) 3.2b, 4.1. and paragraph 59 of the Salary Policy (2009) which reads in part:
All NQTs will be placed on point 1 (M1) of the scale (but cf. the provisions outlined below). One experience point will be awarded for each year of service as a teacher (including any period of approved absence) completed at this or at another school or in an equivalent post e.g. at an Academy, City Technology College, independent school, a maintained overseas school outside the EEA, in a college of FE, a sixth form college, in higher education or at an MOD school.'
My Union advised me to appeal to the Body of governors which I did the same year. According to the School Salary Policy document (2005) which I received when was appointed an appeal is usually lodged on the following grounds - that those making the pay decisions:
• failed to apply the provisions of the STPCD 2008 correctly
• failed to take account of relevant evidence
• failed to have proper regard for statutory guidance
• took account of irrelevant or inaccurate evidence
• were biased or
• discriminated unlawfully against the teacher concerned.(paragraph 51).
After this appeal the Body of Governors endorsed the position of the Head teacher.
I then sought for advice from the Luton Borough Council (HR department) who advised me to keep negotiating with the Head teacher. Unfortunately for me, I had exhausted all forms of negotiation. The HR department informed me also that, if I had evidence that the instrument was being applied inconsistently, then I had a case. I therefore started to investigate the trend among Zimbabwean trained teachers in this region. In a short survey I carried out I found ten (10) teachers in the region who had been placed on the Main Scale at different levels ranging between M3 – M6. Two of the teachers in the statistics above are at Cardinal Newman Secondary School where I teach.
Another set of evidence which shows that the school has discriminated me comes from official records and documents of the school.

The Northampton Religious Education Service
Diocesan Self Evaluation Form (SEF-RE) June 2011
The document referred to above records my experience as beginning on the day I joined Cardinal Newman. It was clear that the school is refusing to recognise my qualifications and experience. I informed the Board of Governors that I was going to make an official complaint to Luton Borough Council that I was unlawfully discriminated against. I also informed the LBC that because the school had failed to apply the provisions of the STPCD 2008 correctly, failed to take account of relevant evidence, and had also failed to have proper regard for statutory guidance, I had been prejudiced financially. I had remained in the same grade in which I was when I joined the school coming from another school two earlier.
At this stage LBC did not respond to my formal complaint. I wrote them again and copied the Head teacher informing them that I was now appealing to the Secretary for Education. The Secretary confirmed that in placing my salary at M3 the Head should have considered my experience as their instrument requires them to. They added that it is up to the Head teacher and the Board of Governors to decide the salary depending on their demands. They however advised me to appeal to the Employment Tribunal.
Employment Tribunal pre-conciliation advised me to proceed with my claim because they could not help me in any way.
Claim: I now submit a claim on the grounds that I was discriminated against. The provisions of their instrument which I quote below were ignored resulting in underpaying me. May I ask you to take note of the difference between paragraphs 3 and 7 which I quote below.

Doc 32 - ET1 Claim of race discrimination p7

Additional information for sections 5.2 and 7.

SCHOOL TEACHERS' SALARY POLICY (2005)
Paragraph 3 states: Starting salary of new appointments:
3.1 The Governing Body has adopted the local agreement in respect of the assessment of teachers' pay. The starting salary for all new entrants to the teachers' pay spine without previous teaching or relevant industrial, professional or research experience will be at point M1.
Paragraph 3.2 also states ' Where the new entrant to the profession has experience which may count towards salary, points will be awarded as follows:
By reference to paragraph 3 (1) above, plus points in respect of teaching service and industrial, professional and research experience considered to be of value in the performance of the teacher's duties on the basis of 1 point in respect of each complete period of 2 years.
Paragraph 4 on Experience also states:
4.1 The Governing Body will award up to six points for experience. A teacher, (including a part time or occasional supply teacher) would be eligible for an experience point for each school year in which the teacher has taught for part of the 26 weeks or was due to but was prevented from doing so for reasons of sickness, maternity or some other absence acknowledged by the Governing Body.
7 RECRUITMENT AND RETENTION ALLOWANCES
7.1 In considering the award of recruitment and retention incentives the Governing Body will have regard for fluctuations in the supply of suitably qualified and experienced teachers. Decisions on the allocation of recruitment and retention incentives will be based on objective evidence. If practicable, the standard advert would run.
These incentives could include any one or combination of the following:
*An incentive to the value of 2.5% of the substantive salary on fixed term basis (maximum duration 3 years)
*Help with removal expenses
*Help with rent
*Provision of a laptop computer
Retention: In the case of shortage subjects or where, in the view of the Head teacher it would be in the interest of the school to retain the services of the member of staff, an award of up to 2.5% of the substantive salary could be made.
I therefore strongly feel that I wrongfully discriminated. The Head teacher might want to argue that those teachers who were correctly placed at M6 after completing QTS were in the advanced skills category. Those that I know in this school were placed on M6 on the basis of paragraph 3 above not even paragraph 7.

Doc 32 - ET1 Claim of race discrimination p8

www.ingramcontent.com/pod-product-compliance
Lightning Source LLC
Chambersburg PA
CBHW030907080526
44589CB00010B/183